Writing Facilitator
Revised Edition

構造から学べるパラグラフ・ライティング入門
改訂版

SHOHAKUSHA

はしがき

　Writing Facilitator は日本人大学生のライティングスキルを無理なく伸ばすための教科書です。その名の通り、ややもすればしきいが高く感じられがちな「パラグラフ・ライティング」を facilitate（易しく）してくれる強力な「支援者」です。

本書の特長

▶▶ パラグラフ構成要素の丁寧な取り扱い

　用語としてのパラグラフ・ライティングはもはや高校生にさえ目新しいものではありません。しかし、よい導入文の特徴、よいトピックセンテンスの書き方、よい結論文の類型、などの細かい点は充分理解されているとは言えません。本書では、個別要素のひな型を具体的に明示することで、望ましいパラグラフが初心者にも必ず書けるような仕組みになっています。

▶▶ プロセスとしてのライティングの重視

　ライティングとは、既に心内に存在する「意味」を単に言語化して表現するだけの行為ではなく、それによって「意味」を整理し、また内容を深化させるような cyclical process（繰り返しのプロセス）です。本書では、Process of Paragraph Writing の項を設け、実際に brain storming で生み出されたアイデアの断片が、どのようなプロセスを経てパラグラフに仕上がるかを実況中継的に提示しています。

▶▶ 身近なトピックからグローバルイッシューまで

　ライティングとは、和文英訳のような第三者から与えられた意味を英語で置き換える作業ではなく、自ら表明したい意思を表現する営みです。日本の大学生には彼（女）らにふさわしい内容があるはずです。本書は「自分の性格」「現在の大学生活」「自分の意見」などの取り組みやすい here-and-now で身近な話題から入り、最終的には「発展途上国の貧困」「絶滅危機動植物」などの 21 世紀に生きる地球市民として誰もが直視すべき global issues を扱います。現代の大学生として「書きたくなる題材」と「書くにふさわしい題材」のバランスを重視しました。

▶▶ 他技能との有機的関連の重視

　ライティングの授業はともすれば個人個人でひたすら書くような単調な授業になりがちです。しかし書いたことは誰かに話したくなるのが当然ですし、逆に聞いたり話したりした経験が書く材料になることもしばしばです。本書は、Talking in Pairs というセクションを設け、書く（あるいは書いた）内容に関連してクラスメートとオーラル・コミュニケーションを行なう機会を出来る限り豊富に設定しています。

▶▶ キーボードによるライティングに対応

　インターネットやパソコンの普及に伴い、現在ライティングはキーボードを入力装置として行なう比率がかなり高くなっています。キーボードライティングをも視野に入れたとき、従来は必要なかったような指導事項が必要になります。ひとつは全角文字と半角文字の関係、もうひとつは punctuation mark と spacing の問題です。本書では従来ほとんど触れられることのなかったこれらの点について丁寧な解説を加え、練習問題を設定しています。

▶▶ 日本的事象に関する、また図やグラフにもとづく発信

　日本人の大学生が将来表現することを求められる可能性の高いトピックのひとつに日本的事象があります。自国の衣食住、生活習慣などについて表現できるようになっておくことはグローバルコミュニティの中でますます重要性が増すでしょう。本書では Unit 10 を日本的事象の表現練習にあて、日本の食習慣、伝統行事などについて簡単に説明できる能力を養います。また Unit 11 ではグラフ、図など視覚情報をもとにしてパラグラフを書く練習をします。いわゆる information transfer の一種でもありますが、将来英語で論文を書くための、基礎訓練にもなります。

▶▶ Focus on Form の重視

　ライティング上達のひとつの鍵はコミュニケーションとしてとにかく大量に書くことです。しかしそれだけでは効率が悪いことが知られており、折にふれ言語形式に意識的に注意を向けることが言語習得には必要と言われています。本書では Focusing on Form として、センテンスレベルの様々なトラブルスポットを取り上げ、editing の練習をする機会を豊富に提供しています。取り上げた英文はすべて大学生が実際に書いたものにもとづいていますので、非常に実用的な editing 練習をすることができます。

◆ まとめ

　本書は、日本人の大学生が、

1. 書きたくなる、あるいは書くにふさわしいような話題について、
2. 聞いたり話したり、という口頭コミュニケーション活動も行ないながら、
3. クラスメートとアドバイスを交換しながら、
4. 英語的なパラグラフとして表現する練習をする

ためのまったく新しいタイプの process writing の教科書です。

　この Writing Facilitator を使って学習するみなさんが、自分の意図を読み手に効果的に伝える力をつけてくれることを祈っています。

2018 年秋

靜　哲人

Contents

はしがき ii

Stage 1 Learning About a Paragraph 1–25

Unit 1
A Paragraph as a Product 2
パラグラフは「段落」じゃない
⋯ *Zenkaku* Characters vs. *Hankaku* Characters

Unit 2
Writing a Topic Sentence 8
主題文で要点を宣言
⋯ Spacing

Unit 3
Writing Supporting Sentences 15
支持文で強力にサポート
⋯ Capitalization

Unit 4
Writing a Concluding Sentence 20
結論文で念押し
⋯ Fragments

The Process of Paragraph Writing 26–33

Stage 2 Writing in a Paragraph Format 34–103

Unit 5
Explaining Your Character 35
自分の性格、好きですか？
⋯ Articles & Nouns

Unit 6
Describing Your Daily Life ······ 43
大学生活は大変？それとも楽チン？
··· Subject-Verb Agreement/Singular vs. Plural

Unit 7
Expressing an Opinion ······ 51
歩きスマホやめてくれない？
··· Tenses

Unit 8
Giving Advice and Instructions ······ 58
ネットショッピング詐欺に引っかからないために
··· Run-Ons

Unit 9
Comparing and Contrasting ······ 65
似て非なるもの：パブと居酒屋
··· Choppiness（I）

Unit 10
Explaining Japanese Culture ······ 73
説明しよう、日本の文化
··· Choppiness（II）

Unit 11
Describing Data Expressed in Graphs ······ 81
データにみる世界の現状
··· Parallel Structure

Unit 12
Summarizing What You Have Read ······ 93
AIによって職が奪われるのか
··· Miscellaneous

Appendix: Additional Cues for Writing ······ 104

Copyright © 2019 by SHIZUKA Tetsuhito
First Published 2019 by Shohakusha Publishing Co., Ltd.
ALL RIGHTS RESERVED. No part of this publication may be reproduced, stored in a retrieval system, transmitted in any form, or by any means, electronic, mechanical, photocopying, recording, or otherwise, without the prior written permission of the publishers.

Photo Acknowledgments

p. 1: © BIGANDT.COM ／ p. 2:（上段左）© Happy monkey;（上段右）© Keisuke_N;（下段左）© Photo-SD;（下段中）© KPG_Payless;（下段右）© Alena Ozerova ／ p. 8:（左）© garagestock;（右）© Elena11 ／ p. 15:（左）© MMpai;（右上）© Photographee.eu;（右下）© iGuide ／ p. 20:（左）© MIA Studio;（右上）© GagliardiImages;（右下）© maroke ／ p. 34 : © vectorfusionart ／ p. 35:（左列上）© fizkes;（左列下）© Iakov Filimonov/ Halfpoint;（中列上）© Twinsterphoto ;（中列下）© Pressmaster;（右列上）© WAYHOME studio;（右列中）© LightField Studios;（右列下）© Antonio Guillem ／ p. 43:（上段左）© Ioan Florin Cnejevici;（上段右）© ESB Professional;（下段左）© 4 PM production;（下段中）© LightField Studios;（下段右）© Geoff Goldswain ／ p. 51:（左上）© Cat Box;（左下）© antoniodiaz;（右）© stockfour ／ p. 58:（左上）© Shamleen;（左下）© fizkes;（右）© fizkes ／ p. 65:（上段左）© Anutr Yossundara;（上段中）© taa22;（上段右）© Diego Cervo;（下段左）© icosha;（下段中）© Lucian Milasan;（下段右）© Bikeworldtravel ／ p. 73:（上段左）© Nishihama;（上段中）© Soundaholic studio;（上段右）© Vassamon Anansukkasem;（下段左）© IZO;（下段中）© jazz3311;（下段右）© gori910 / okimo ／ p. 81:（上段左）© michaeljung;（上段右）© Riccardo Mayer;（下段左）© smolaw;（下段中）© AveNa;（下段右）© Pressmaster ／ p. 93:（左）© Alexander Raths;（右上）© Zapp2Photo;（右下）© Matej Kastelic

Stage 1

Learning About a Paragraph

You are going to learn . . .

what exactly a paragraph is	(Unit 1);
how to write topic sentences	(Unit 2);
how to write supporting sentences	(Unit 3); and
how to write concluding sentences	(Unit 4).

UNIT 1

A Paragraph as a Product
パラグラフは「段落」じゃない

言語にはそれぞれ固有の論理展開があります。この Unit では英語の論理展開の基本的パタンを学習しましょう。

複数のセンテンスがまとまってひとつのアイデアを表現しているものをパラグラフ (paragraph) と呼びます。パラグラフは次のような形をしています。

Why English Is Important

It is important for us to learn English for at least three reasons. First, English is almost always useful to communicate with someone who does not understand Japanese. It is estimated that more than a billion people in the whole world understand English. Second, someone with good English skills will have wider choices of future jobs. Most companies today are requiring new employees to have high English skills. Finally, knowing English will make such a big difference in the amount of information we can access. Since English is now the standard language on the Internet, almost every piece of information from outside Japan first comes in English. Indeed, English is a language worth learning seriously.

Task 1-1

上のパラグラフの中で、…
(1) 全体の内容をまとめて書いているセンテンスはいくつありますか。そのようなセンテンスに下線を引きましょう。
(2) (1)で下線を引いたセンテンスが述べている内容の根拠は、大きく分けていくつ挙げられていますか。それぞれの根拠を述べる部分が始まる最初の語に○をつけましょう。

Task 1-2

上のパラグラフの最初と最後のセンテンスの関係は、次のうちどれですか。
A. The two sentences are exactly the same; saying the same thing using the same wording.
B. The two sentences are saying two different things; the latter introduces a new topic.
C. The two sentences are saying almost the same thing using slightly different words.

Task 1-3

次の用語について音声もしくは先生の説明を聞き、要点をメモしましょう。

▶▶ indentation

▶▶ topic sentence

▶▶ supporting sentences

▶▶ concluding sentence

Task 1-4

p. 3 のパラグラフの ...
(1) indentation が起こっている部分にチェックをつけ、
(2) topic sentence の最初に TS と書き、
(3) それぞれの major point が始まるセンテンスの最初に、MP1, MP2, ... と書き、
(4) concluding sentence の最初に CS と書きましょう。

NOTE: concluding sentence を持たないパラグラフも現実には多くありますが、本書では、最も基本となるフォーマットを繰り返し練習するという意味で、パラグラフには topic sentence とともに、必ず concluding sentence をつけることにします。

Task 1-5

パラグラフは一見、日本語の文章の「段落」の英語版のようですが、その構成は大きく違います。音声あるいは先生の説明を聞き、要点をメモしましょう。

an English paragraph	a Japanese danraku

Task 1-6

次の A, B では、どちらが英語らしいパラグラフか選びましょう。

A Japanese students in English classes should spend more time producing English. The only way to improve one's command of a foreign language is to use it as much as possible. Even when you read an English passage, if you explain its meaning only in Japanese, your ability to speak English will never get better. However, in many English classes, the students are only required to translate English into Japanese. That is why most Japanese English learners fail to become reasonably good English speakers. In order to change the situation, students in English classes should be encouraged to explain things in English.

B Most Japanese English learners fail to become reasonably good English speakers. Why is this? The only way to improve one's command of a foreign language is to use it as much as possible. However, in many English classes, the students are only required to translate English into Japanese. Even when you read an English passage, if you only explain its meaning in Japanese, your ability to speak English will never get better. Therefore, in order to change the situation, students in English classes should be encouraged to explain things in English.

Task 1-7

次のセンテンスが英語らしいパラグラフを構成するためには、どのような順番が最も適切か考えましょう。解答は音声を聞いて確認しましょう。

A) A lot of wild animals are killed so that their body parts can be made into various products.
B) Buying or using such products is virtually the same as killing the animals.
C) I believe people who wear fur coats, crocodile belts, or tortoiseshell accessories should know better.
D) If buying stops, killing will, too.
E) One of the major causes is illegal hunting.
F) Poachers hunt these animals because there are people who buy such products.
G) Therefore, we should never buy products made from wild animals.
H) Today, the list of endangered animals is getting longer and longer.

📖 Focusing on Form

Zenkaku Characters vs. *Hankaku* Characters

PCのキーボードに慣れていない人がタイプした英語は、つぎのような外観になることがあります。

Ｔｏｄａｙ，　ａ　ｌｏｔ　ｏｆ　ｐｅｏｐｌｅ　ｋｅｅｐ　ｐｅｔｓ．Ｔｈｅ　ｔｗｏ　ｍｏｓｔ　ｃｏｍｍｏｎ　ｐｅｔ　ａｎｉｍａｌｓ　ａｒｅ　ｃａｔｓ　ａｎｄ　ｄｏｇｓ．　Ｂｏｔｈ　ａｒｅ　ｑｕｉｔｅ　ｐｏｐｕｌａｒ，　ｂｕｔ　ｔｈｅｒｅ　ａｒｅ　ｓｏｍｅ　ｉｍｐｏｒｔａｎｔ　ｄｉｆｆｅｒｅｎｃｅｓ　ｂｅｔｗｅｅｎ　ｔｈｅ　ｔｗｏ　ａｎｉｍａｌｓ．

これは日本語のフォントの「全角文字」で打った英文字です。見かけは英語のようですが、実はコンピュータは英語と認識してくれません。例えばマウスで選択して別の英語フォントに変えようと思っても変わりません。この「英文」を日本語フォントのないパソコンに送信すると文字化けしてしまいます。また、妙に横に間延びして、しかも行の右端を見ると単語の途中のあらぬところ（音節の切れ目以外の場所）で改行されてしまうことがあります。このような英語を打たないようにしましょう。

英語は英語のフォント（Times New Roman とか Century など）を使って「半角文字」（1バイト文字とも言う）で打つ必要があり、正しくは次のような外観になります。

Today a lot of people keep pets. The two most common pet animals are cats and dogs. Both are quite popular, but there are some important differences between the two animals.

これに関連して、以下の点も覚えておいてください。

- ✓ 行の一番右にいっても改行記号を入れ（つまり、リターンキーを押し）てはいけません。改行はパソコンが自動的にしてくれます。自分で改行記号を入れてよいのはパラグラフの最後だけです。

- ✓ 単語が行の切れ目にかかりそうになると、パソコンが自動的にその語全体を次の行に送ってくれます。よってパソコンで打っている時は、わざわざ自分でハイフンを入れて単語の途中で改行する必要はありません。

- ✓ 手書きの場合にも、ハイフンを入れる正しい位置（音節の切れ目）を辞書なしで知るのは至難の技です。よって、どんな場合にも語の途中では改行せず、行の右端が多少デコボコになっても、単語ごと次行から始めるのがもっとも安全で確実な方法です。

UNIT

2

Writing a Topic Sentence
主題文で要点を宣言

この Unit では topic sentence についてさらに深く学び、良い topic sentence を書く練習をします。

Unit 1 では、topic sentence については、およそ次のような説明がなされました。

The topic sentence of a paragraph presents the main idea of the paragraph.

Task 2-1

◉ CD 08   ⬇ DL 08

録音されている音声を聞き、
(1) main idea に必要な 2 つの要素をメモしましょう。
(2) A ～ F が、topic sentence として良いか悪いかチェックしましょう。

a main idea = [　　　　　　　　　] + [　　　　　　　　　　　　]

A) I am going to write about how I spend my free time.　　　　[　　]
B) The topic of my paragraph is music.　　　　　　　　　　　　[　　]
C) I spend my free time mostly by listening to music.　　　　　　[　　]
D) My favorite way of spending free time is listening to music.　[　　]
E) I usually spend my free time listening to my favorite songs.　[　　]
F) How do you spend your free time?　　　　　　　　　　　　　[　　]

Task 2-2

1. ～ 4. のパラグラフには topic sentence がありません。topic sentence として最も適当なものをそれぞれ A ～ C から選びましょう。自分の答えが決まったらクラスメートと確認してみましょう。

1. _____ First, dogs bark a lot while cats do not make sounds very often. Second, dogs can enjoy traveling with their owners, but cats prefer staying in the familiar house. Third, dogs can be trained to do some tricks, which is impossible with cats.

A) Cats and dogs are both popular pets, but there are some important differences between them.
B) Today, the number of cats kept as pets in Japan is larger than that of dogs.
C) Though people keep some exotic pets nowadays, cats and dogs are still the most popular.

2. _____ First, it should be relatively close to the campus. It should not take more than thirty minutes. In addition, the rent should not be too expensive. It has to be ¥45,000 or less. Finally, the apartment house should not be too old or dirty. I do not want to be embarrassed when my friends come over.

A) There are many things I have to consider when choosing an apartment.
B) I am going to write about how to choose a good apartment.
C) When you choose an apartment, what is important to you?

3. _____ First of all, you can look up words much more quickly in electronic dictionaries. This means that you will look up words much more frequently. Another advantage is that electronic dictionaries are much lighter. You can carry one wherever you go. Moreover, some electronic dictionaries let you do what you cannot possibly do with a paper dictionary. For example, you can make a list of all the example sentences containing a word you designate.

A) Although portable electronic dictionaries are useful, they are much more expensive than printed ones.
B) Portable electronic dictionaries have advantages as well as disadvantages.
C) Portable electronic dictionaries have several advantages over printed dictionaries.

4. _____ The biggest advantage is that apps are easier to carry around. You can use them as long as you have your smartphones on you. Unlike smartphones, you do not carry e-dictionaries at all times. Another advantage is that key responses tend to feel faster on apps than on e-dictionaries. Once you get used to apps, e-dictionaries can feel a bit slow. A disadvantage is that it is not always as easy to jump from one dictionary app to another dictionary app. An e-dictionary lets you access multiple dictionaries quite seamlessly. The biggest disadvantage is that you can be misunderstood. When you are using a dictionary app in class, your teacher can get offended believing that you are texting or surfing the net.

A) In my opinion, e-dictionaries have a big advantage over dictionary apps on smartphones.

B) Dictionary apps on smartphones, compared to stand-alone e-dictionaries, have both advantages and disadvantages.

C) Dictionary apps on smartphones are more effective than traditional stand-alone e-dictionaries.

Task 2-3

1.～3. のパラグラフには topic sentence がありません。supporting sentences をよく読んで、適当な topic sentence の例を書いてみましょう。

1. _____ A few instructors are really terrible. They come fifteen minutes late to class, and leave ten minutes early. Their lectures are so boring that half of us are sleeping. I doubt that they care if we understand them or not. Though we want to let them know that we are not happy with their classes, to say that to their faces would be difficult. There is no other way than conducting a class survey.

2. _____ First, the campus is in a wonderful location. It is on a hill, commanding a view of the whole city. The view is superb especially in the evening. Second, the faculty is outstanding. Most professors have PhDs and are leading researchers in their respective fields. Third, the university is very strong in job placement. The alumni network is quite strong so that we will be in an advantageous position to find jobs we want.

3. _____ The campus is on a hill, commanding a view of the whole city. On a clear day, you can see beautiful mountains far away. The sense of vast space is truly valuable. The view is superb especially in the evening; city lights gleam like diamonds. On the other hand, the downside is that there are no restaurants or shops nearby. When you come to this campus, you have to bring from town everything you need for the day. In addition, it takes more than 25 minutes by bus from the nearest station.

Task 2-4

4人程度のグループで、Task 2-3 で各人が書いた topic sentence を比較検討しましょう。

Task 2-5

Topic sentence の前に introductory sentences をもってくることがあります。Introductory sentences は、非常に一般的 (general) な statement から始め、無理なく topic sentence の内容につながるように書きます。

Example

Today, a lot of people keep pets. The two most common pet animals are cats and dogs. Both are quite popular, but there are some important differences between the two animals.

分析してみると次のようになっています。

Today, a lot of people keep pets.
<very general>

The two most common pet animals are cats and dogs.
<somewhat specific>

Both are quite popular, but there are some important
differences between the two animals.
<topic sentence>

次の文が topic sentence である場合に、読者をそこまで導く introductory sentences を書いてみましょう。

1. The way people communicate with each other has changed a lot in these thirty years.

2. Today, no governments can afford to ignore NGOs.

3. Students can learn a lot of valuable lessons from working part-time.

📖 Focusing on Form

Spacing

手書きの時はそれほど問題になりませんが、キーボードを使って英語を打つ際には、スペースの用い方に関する次のルールを守らねばなりません。

Rule 1   原則として punctuation marks（句読記号）は、直前の語のすぐ後に（スペースで隔てずに）置く。
  - ✕   What do you think of my opinion ?
  - ○   What do you think of my opinion?

Rule 2   原則として punctuation marks の後には、スペースを１つ置く。
  - ✕   In my opinion,his argument was rather weak.The judge was not convinced.
  - ○   In my opinion, his argument was rather weak. The judge was not convinced.

  * **Rule 2 の例外**　略号の内部に用いるピリオド（例えば、"U.S.A." の最初の２つのピリオド）の後にはスペースを置かない。アポストロフィの後にも置かない。
  - ✕   The session started at 9 a. m. and ended at 2 p. m.
  - ○   The session started at 9 a.m. and ended at 2 p.m.

Rule 3   quotation marks (" "), brackets (( )) などの場合には、それらの囲みの中の要素との間にはスペースを置かない。囲みの外の要素との間にはスペースを１つ置く。
  - ✕   World Wildlife Fund(WWF)is addressing conservation issues.
  - ○   World Wildlife Fund (WWF) is addressing conservation issues.

Rule 4   ハイフン (-)、ダッシュ (—) の前後にはスペースを置かない。（なお、ダッシュは２つの連続したハイフンとしてタイプすればよい。）

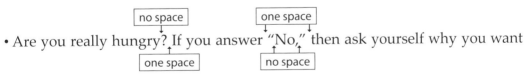

- Are you really hungry? If you answer "No," then ask yourself why you want

to eat when your body is not really hungry.

- They chose one ten-millionth (1/10,000,000) of the distance from the Equator

to the North Pole.

- Because there are no written records, we can't be certain. However, there is one interesting fact.
  - one space (after comma following records)
  - one space (after period following certain)
  - no space (before comma after However)

Now *you* try!

次の文の spacing が適切になるように修正しましょう。本来スペースをとるべきところにスペースがない場合には ∨∧、スペースをとるべきでないところにスペースがある場合には ∧∨ という記号を付してください。

1. Although people talk about the Kansai dialect , Osaka dialect, Kyoto dialect , and Kobe dialect are different from each other.

2. In my opinion , non-governmental organizations (NGOs) have a lot of important roles to play in today's international community. What do you think ?

3. The president said at the press conference , "We will not rule out any means in order to uproot terrorists . "

UNIT

3

Writing Supporting Sentences
支持文で強力にサポート

このUnitではSupporting Sentencesの書き方について、さらに詳しく学習します。

Unit 1 では、supporting sentences については、おおよそ次のような説明がなされました。

The topic sentence should be supported by the rest of the sentences in the paragraph, which are called supporting sentences. Supporting sentences usually present several major points.

Task 3-1　　　　　　　　　　　　　　　　　　　　CD 09　　DL 09

音声もしくは先生の説明を聞き、良い supporting sentences の特徴をメモしましょう。

Task 3-2

A)〜C) のパラグラフには supporting sentences として不適当なものが含まれています。どの文が不適当なのかを見極め、なぜ不適当なのか説明しましょう。

A)　There are several reasons why you usually cannot keep pets in apartments. Some pets make loud noises, which will disturb families next door. Some are dangerous. Large dogs can be a real threat to small children. In addition, some pets can damage the rooms. Stains on tatami mats or scratches on the floor will lower the value of the property. However, the number of apartments that allow pets is on the rise.

B) Being a university student is a tough business. You need to spend many hours preparing for your classes. In order to attend one 90-minute session, you need to prepare about two hours. The attendance policy is strict, so you need to attend almost all the classes. The teachers say that if we miss three classes, we are "out," just like in a baseball game. This is a bad rule because the rule is treating us just like high school students.

C) Shohaku University is popular among students mainly for three reasons. First, the facilities are excellent. All classrooms are clean and air-conditioned. State-of-the-art PCs are available 24 hours a day. As a result, the tuition is one of the highest in Japan, which is a drawback. Second, there are a number of distinguished scholars on the faculty. It is exciting to learn from leading researchers in respective fields. The most important reason, however, is its location. Since it is right in the middle of downtown, students can fully enjoy their social lives.

Task 3-3

次のtopic sentenceに対するsupporting sentencesを、それぞれ3つ書いてみましょう。

1. You should be careful about several things when using social media.

   - _____
   - _____
   - _____

2. Smartphones are an indispensable tool in our lives.

   - _____
   - _____
   - _____

3. Several things have surprised me since I entered this university.

   - _____
   - _____
   - _____

4. Big cities attract young people for several reasons.

   - _____
   - _____
   - _____

5. It is important for us to acquire basic computer skills.

   - _____
   - _____
   - _____

Focusing on Form

Capitalization

大文字の使用に関して、これまでよく知っているものの他に、ここでは**タイトル**に使用するときのルールを覚えましょう。

Rule 1 すべての「主要な」語は大文字で始める。冠詞、前置詞、接続詞以外のすべての語は「主要な」語である。
Rule 2 品詞にかかわらず、4文字以上の語は「主要な」語と見なし、大文字で始める。
Rule 3 品詞にかかわらず、タイトルの最初の語は大文字で始める。

＊なお、タイトルは通常中央揃え（centering）にします。

Now *you* try!

パラグラフのタイトルとして適切になるよう、必要な文字を大文字にしましょう。

1. a person I respect

2. my most unforgettable experience

3. why I believe we need more elective subjects

4. how best to choose a vacation spot

5. the problem of illegal parking about the campus

6. tips for enjoying college life

UNIT

4

Writing a Concluding Sentence
結論文で念押し

このUnitでは、効果的なConcluding Sentenceの書き方を練習します。

Unit 1 では、concluding sentence については、おおよそ次のような説明がなされました。

The concluding sentence of a paragraph restates the main idea, using somewhat different words from the topic sentence.

Unit 1 での最初のモデルパラグラフ (p. 3) の topic sentence (TS) と concluding sentence (CS) は、それぞれ以下のようでした。
TS: It is important for us to learn English for at least three reasons.
CS: Indeed, English is a language worth learning seriously.

Task 4-1

先生の説明あるいは音声を聞いて、concluding sentence を書く際のコツについてメモしましょう。

Technique 1: _____

    Example _____

Technique 2: _____

    Example _____

Technique 3: _____

    Example _____

Concluding Phrases:
_____
_____

Task 4-2

1～9の topic sentence に対応する concluding sentence を、それぞれ Technique 1 (T1) によって2つ、Technique 3 (T3) によって1つ、書いてみましょう。

1. An English paragraph is different from a Japanese *danraku* in several important ways.
   - → T1: _____
   - → T1: _____
   - → T3: _____

2. Smartphones have become an indispensable tool for many people's lives.
   - → T1: _____
   - → T1: _____
   - → T3: _____

3. iPhones have several advantages over Android phones.
   - → T1: _____
   - → T1: _____
   - → T3: _____

4. Professor S's English classes are demanding in many ways.
   - → T1: _____
   - → T1: _____
   - → T3: _____

5. Our generation and our parents' generation have very different ideas about marriage.
   - → T1: _____
   - → T1: _____
   - → T3: _____

6. One of the key concepts that companies need to promote is diversity.
   - → T1: _____
   - → T1: _____
   - → T3: _____

7. I chose to enter this university for three main reasons.
   - → T1: _____
   - → T1: _____
   - → T3: _____

8. When you are a university student, it is very difficult to keep regular hours.
   - → T1: _____
   - → T1: _____
   - → T3: _____

9. Working part-time is a precious experience that helps me learn a lot of new things.
   - → T1: _____
   - → T1: _____
   - → T3: _____

Task 4-3

次は、Task 4-2のtopic sentenceに対応して学生が書いたconcluding sentenceですが、誤りを含むものもあるようです。誤りがある場合には直してみましょう。

1. In these way, an English paragraph differs from a Japanese danraku.

2. In brief, smartphones cannot do without about many people.

3. Indeed, students in Professor S's class need to work hard.

Task 4-4

(1) 4人程度のグループで、Task 4-2 で各人が書いた concluding sentence を比較検討しましょう。
(2) 1〜9のそれぞれについて、グループ内の、Technique 1, Technique 3 による最優秀 concluding sentence を決めましょう。
(3) グループごとに最優秀 concluding sentence を発表し、クラス内の最優秀作を決めましょう。

Focusing on Form

Fragments

それだけでは独立したセンテンスにならないのに、大文字で始めてピリオド等で終え、センテンスのような外観にしてしまっているものを、**fragments**（破片）と呼びます。fragments は誤りです。日本人学習者がつい書きがちである fragments の代表的なものに、次のようなもの（下線部）があります。

a. I don't think English should be taught to children in the lower grades at primary school in Japan. <u>Because they need to learn Japanese first</u>.
b. Recent news about school is rather depressing. <u>For example, bullying, suicide, and violence</u>.

それぞれ次のように修正してセンテンスにする必要があります。

a'-1. I don't think English should be taught to children in the lower grades at primary school in Japan **because** they need to learn Japanese first.
a'-2. I don't think English should be taught at primary school in Japan. **That is because** children need to learn Japanese first.

b'-1. Recent news about schools is rather depressing. **For example, there are** a lot of reports on bullying, suicide, and violence.
b'-2. Recent news about schools–**bullying, suicide, and violence, for example**–is rather depressing.

Now *you* try!

1～4の文章中の fragments を見つけて、正しく直しましょう。

1. My pet is a female dog. One of my precious family members.

   _____

2. Only one life, no regret. Therefore, I hope to experience many things.

   _____

3. I believe working part-time is very important. Because we can learn a lot of things about the real world. For example, the importance of punctuality.

   _____

   _____

4. In my free time, I usually do something related to movies. For example, going to the movie theater, studying movie scenarios, and browsing movie websites. Because I want to be a subtitle translator in the future.

   _____

   _____

   _____

The Process of Paragraph Writing

これまでは product（完成品）としてのパラグラフの構成を学習してきました。しかしパラグラフは一気に product として完成するわけではありません。普通、次のような process（過程）を経て作られるのです。

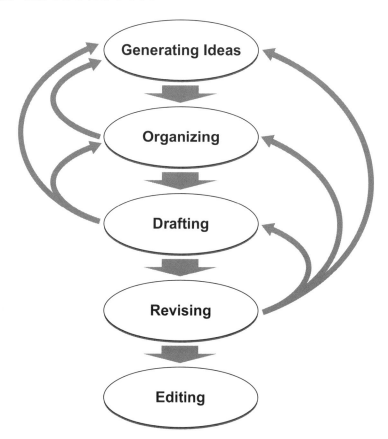

Generating Ideas

パラグラフを書くためには、まず書く材料がなければなりません。書くべき材料を考え出す（generate する）のがこの作業です。そのためには、あるトピックについて思いつくことをどんどんメモしてゆくのが効果的です。この段階では、順番、重要度の差、英語表現の正確さなどはあまり気にせず、思いつくままに出来る限りたくさんメモするのがコツです。この作業は Brain Storming とも呼ばれます。

Example 1 Clustering

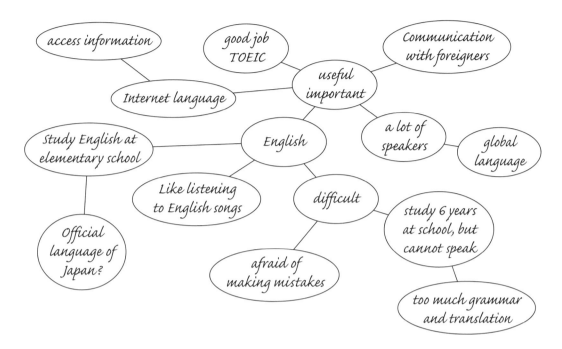

Example 2 Listing

English
useful, important
difficult
study many years at school, but cannot speak
too much grammar and translation
like listening to English songs
afraid of making mistakes
good job, TOEIC
Internet language
access information
communication with foreigners
English-speaking visitors from overseas
a lot of speakers
global language
study English at elementary school
official language of Japan?

Task 1

次のトピック（あるいは自分の好きなトピック）からひとつ選び、思いつくideaを、英語（または日本語）で出来る限りたくさん、3分間で書いてみましょう。

- What Kind of Person I Am
- What I Like to Do in My Free Time
- What I Like About This University
- What I Do Not Like About This University

Organizing

思いつきをすべて並べたのでは、第三者に理解しやすいパラグラフは書けません。パラグラフに含める内容の構成を整えるのがOrganizingです。Generating Ideasでリストアップしたideasの中から、まず中心となる命題、main ideaを決めます。その後で、ideasの中から、main ideaをサポートするために使えるものだけを選びます。

今仮にmain ideaをIt is important to learn English.だとすると、サポートとして使えそうなのは次のものです。

English
useful, important
~~difficult~~
~~study many years at school, but cannot speak~~
~~too much grammar and translation~~
~~like listening to English songs~~
~~afraid of making mistakes~~
~~should enjoy speaking~~
good job, TOEIC
Internet language
access information
communication with foreigners
English-speaking visitors from overseas
a lot of speakers
global language
~~study English at elementary school~~
~~official language of Japan?~~

残った ideas を使い、次のような形でパラグラフの骨組みを表わしたものを Outline と呼びます。

> Main Idea: It is important to learn English.
> 1. useful to communicate with non-Japanese English-speaking visitors from overseas
> 2. wider choices of future jobs more companies require English skills
> 3. can access a lot of information standard language on the Web

TASK 2

もし、main idea が、In English classes, we should practice speaking more. だとしたら、どうでしょうか。
(1) その場合に使える ideas を選んでみましょう。
(2) 残った ideas を、いくつかのポイントに構成して Outline の形にしてみましょう。

English
useful, important
difficult
study many years at school, but cannot speak
too much grammar and translation
like listening to English songs
afraid of making mistakes
should enjoy speaking
good job, TOEIC
Internet language
access information
communication with foreigners
English-speaking visitors from overseas
a lot of speakers
global language
study English at elementary school
official language of Japan?

このように、何を main idea にするかによって、パラグラフに含めるべき supporting ideas は変わってきます。逆に言えば、含めたい supporting ideas によって、main idea を変えなければならないのです。

Task 3

Task 1 で自分がリストアップした ideas を眺め、
(1) main idea をひとつ決め、
(2) その main idea をサポートする ideas だけを選び、
(3) 選んだ ideas を、Outline の形に構成してみましょう。

Drafting

Outline ができたら、それをとりあえず英語にしてみましょう。この段階では、英語表現に悩むよりは、全体の構成がしっかりしているかどうかに意識を集中することが大切です。（この点を強調するため、以下の Task で提示している sample drafts では、最終稿に至るまでは、**英語表現が不充分な点を敢えて残しています。**）

Task 4

Task 3 で作った Outline にそって、Draft 1（第1稿）を書いてみましょう。

Draft 1 **Example**

　　It is important to learn English. English is useful to communicate with non-Japanese people. English-speaking visitors from overseas are everywhere. English will give you wider choice of future job. More and more companies are requiring English skills. If you understand English, you can access a lot of informations. English is standard language on Web.

Rivising

Draft 1 ができたら、まず内容面、全体の構成に意識を向けて眺めてみましょう。上の例では、introductory sentences と、concluding sentences を補うことにします。（この2つは不可欠な要素ではありませんが、ここでは補うことにしてみます。）

Draft 2 **Example**

　　Japan is getting more serious about learning English. Public schools are offering English classes for longer years. I believe this is good trend because it is important to learn English.　English is useful in communicating with non-Japanese people.　English-speaking visitors from overseas are everywhere. English will give you wider choice of future job.　More and more companies are requiring English skills.　If you understand English, you can access a lot of informations.　English is standard language on Web.　For these reasons, English is worth learning.　If you keep this in mind and work hard, you will be good English speaker.

TASK 5

Draft 1 (**Example**) と Draft 2 (**Example**) を見比べ、Draft 2 で加筆修正された部分に下線を引いて確認してみましょう。

TASK 6

Task 4 で書いた自分の Draft 1 を revise して Draft 2 にしてみましょう。（クラスメートと交換してお互いの draft を見るのも大変有効な方法です。）

Further Rivising

Draft 2 をもう一度見て、内容的にさらに加筆、修正、削除が必要であれば書き直します。次の例では、つなぎ言葉を補い、またいくつかの個所で表現を修正しました。

Draft 3 **Example**

　　Today it seems that Japan as nation is getting more serious about learning English. Public schools are offering English classes for longer years and people who go to private conversation schools seem to be on the rise.　I believe this is good trend because it is important to learn English for at least three reasons. First, English is useful in communicating with non-Japanese people.　English-speaking visitors from overseas can be found in almost any sightseeing spot today.　Second, English will give you wider choice of future job.　More and more companies are requiring new employee to have good English skills.　The higher your TOEIC score is, the more likely you will get promoted.　Finally, if you understand English, you can access a lot of information from overseas firsthand. Since English is standard language on Web, whether or not you can read English will make big difference in what information is available to you. For these reasons, English is clearly worth learning. If you keep this in mind and work hard, you will surely be good English speaker.

TASK 7

Draft 2 (**Example**) と Draft 3 (**Example**) を見比べて、Draft 3 で加筆修正された部分に下線を引いて確認しましょう。

Editing

Draft 3 をもう一度、今度は英語表現上の細かい問題がないかを中心に検討し、加筆・修正をします。この例では、冠詞が抜けている箇所や、単数・複数のミスが発見されたので直しました。

Final Draft **Example**

Three Reasons Why English Is Worth Learning

  Today it seems that Japan as a nation is getting more serious about learning English. Public schools are offering English classes for longer years and people who go to private conversation schools seem to be on the rise. I believe this is a good trend because it is important to learn English for at least three reasons. First, English is useful in communicating with non-Japanese people. English-speaking visitors from overseas can be found in almost any sightseeing spot today. Second, English will give you wider choices of future jobs. More and more companies are requiring new employees to have good English skills. After being employed, the higher their TOEIC score is, the more likely they will get promoted. Finally, if you understand English, you can access a lot of information from overseas firsthand. Since English is the standard language on the Web, whether or not you can read English will make a big difference in what information is available to you. For these reasons, English is clearly worth learning seriously. If you keep this in mind and work hard, you will surely be a good English speaker.

Task 8

Draft 3 (**Example**) と、Final Draft (**Example**) を見比べて、Final Draft で加筆修正された部分に下線を引いて確認しましょう。

Task 9

自分の Draft 2 をもう一度点検し、表現上のミスをできる限りなくして、Final Draft を作ってみましょう。（クラスメート同士で draft を交換して editing をする peer editing も非常に有効な方法です。）

» まとめ

ライティングは、一度書いて終わるのではなく、時間の許す限り revising と editing を繰り返して draft の完成度を高めてゆく、繰り返しのプロセス (a cyclical process) です。またその際、まず内容面、構成面に注意を集中して大枠を固めてから、次に文法ミスや表現の改善などの表層に注意を移す、という順番が大切です。もちろん文法ミスに気づいたならその時点で直せばよいのですが、木を見て森を見ず、ということになってはいけません。

Rule 1   *Writing is a cyclical process.*

Rule 2   *Organization first; grammar and mechanics later.*

Stage 2

Writing in a Paragraph Format

You are going to learn... write paragraphs that

explain your character	(Unit 5);
describe your daily life	(Unit 6);
express your opinion	(Unit 7);
give advice and instructions	(Unit 8);
compare and contrast two things	(Unit 9);
explain Japanese culture	(Unit 10);
describe data expressed in graphs	(Unit 11); and
summarize what you have read	(Unit 12).

UNIT 5

Explaining Your Character

自分の性格、好きですか？

このUnitでは自分の性格を説明するパラグラフを書きましょう。

Task 5-1 Generating Ideas

次の性格スケール上で、自分がいると思う位置にそれぞれ○をつけましょう。

extremely	very	rather	not very	not at all	
5	4	3	2	1	optimistic
5	4	3	2	1	hardworking
5	4	3	2	1	ambitious
5	4	3	2	1	easy-going
5	4	3	2	1	sociable
5	4	3	2	1	competitive
5	4	3	2	1	organized
5	4	3	2	1	confident
5	4	3	2	1	dependable
5	4	3	2	1	jealous
5	4	3	2	1	patient
5	4	3	2	1	talkative
5	4	3	2	1	lazy
5	4	3	2	1	energetic
5	4	3	2	1	creative
5	4	3	2	1	shy
5	4	3	2	1	thrifty
5	4	3	2	1	artistic
5	4	3	2	1	outgoing
5	4	3	2	1	brave
5	4	3	2	1	honest
5	4	3	2	1	responsible
5	4	3	2	1	sensitive
5	4	3	2	1	serious

Task 5-2　Writing a Topic Sentence

p. 36 のスケールで、○をつけた位置が最も左であった語を３つ選び、次の _____ に書きましょう。

I am a(n) _____ , _____ , and _____ person.

これが main idea のもとになります。今回の topic sentence は次のようにします。

I can describe my character fairly well using three adjectives.

Task 5-3　Writing Introductory Sentences

Topic sentence に読者を導くための introductory sentences を書きましょう。topic sentence よりも general な内容で始め、topic sentence につながるよう工夫します。

Example

Different people have different characters. <general>

In Japan it is commonly believed that people's personalities have something to do with their blood types. <specific>

Whether or not this is true, [I can describe my character fairly well using three adjectives.]

Task 5-4　Outlining

Task 5-2 で選んだ３つの形容詞それぞれについて、その性格の実例となるようなことがらをそれぞれ、メモの形で書いてみましょう。

Example

1. optimistic … rarely worry / ex. entrance examination
2. sociable … enjoy meeting new people / never miss parties
3. artistic … love music / playing piano for fifteen years

Task 5-5 Writing Supporting Sentences

Task 5-4 でたてたポイントのひとつひとつを、それぞれ 2 つのセンテンスで表現しましょう。最初のセンテンスは、比較的 general に、2 番目のセンテンスは比較的 specific な内容にします。

Example

1. optimistic … rarely worry / ex. entrance examination
   - I am optimistic because I rarely worry about things in the future. <general>
   - When I was preparing for university entrance examinations, the only thing I had in mind was how I was going to enjoy my college life. <specific>

2. sociable … enjoy meeting new people / never miss parties
   - I am a sociable person who enjoys meeting new people. <general>
   - I never miss parties even when a report is due the next day. <specific>

3. artistic … love music / playing piano for fifteen years
   - I am an artistic person who cannot live without music. <general>
   - I have been playing the piano almost every day for 15 years. <specific>

Task 5-6 Talking in Pairs

Task 5-5 で書いた outline を利用して、ペアで話す練習をしてみましょう。

Example

A: How do you describe your character?
B: Well, first of all, I am optimistic.
A: Optimistic? In what way?
B: I rarely worry about things in the future.
A: I see.
B: I am also sociable.
A: Can you give me an example?
B: I enjoy meeting new people. I never miss drinking parties.
A: Really?
B: Yeah. And lastly, I am artistic.

A: Artistic in what way?
B: I love music. I have been playing the piano for fifteen years.
A: So, you are optimistic, sociable, and artistic.
B: That's right. Now it's your turn. How do you describe your character?
A: Well, ...

Task 5-7 ▸ Writing Concluding Sentences

Unit 4 で学んだ3つのテクニークで、concluding sentence を書いてみましょう。

Example

Technique 1 (Restating the topic sentence):
Thus, these three adjectives will give you a fairly accurate image about what kind of person I am.

Technique 2 (Summarizing the main points):
To summarize, I am living a life without worries, surrounded by a lot of friends, and enriched by music.

Technique 3 (Giving a final thought):
I hope to stay this way because I like my character.

Task 5-8 ▸ Putting It All Together

いままで書いた文を改めてパラグラフにまとめましょう。構成を明確にするためのつなぎ言葉も使いましょう。

Example

Words That Best Describe My Character

Different people have different characters. In Japan it is commonly believed that people's personalities have something to do with their blood types. Whether or not this is true, I can describe my character fairly well using three adjectives. **First of all**, I should say that I am optimistic because I rarely worry about things in the future. When I was preparing for university entrance examinations, the only thing I had in mind was how I was going to enjoy my college life. I am **also** a sociable person who enjoys meeting new people. That is why I never miss parties even when a report is due the next day. **Lastly**, I am an artistic person who cannot live without music. Actually, I have been playing the piano almost every day for 15 years. **To summarize**, I am living a life without worries, surrounded by a lot of friends, and enriched by music. I hope to stay this way because I like my character.

Words That Best Describe My Character

_____

_____ I can describe my character fairly

well using three adjectives. First of all, I should say that I am _____

because I _____

_____

I am also a(n) _____ person who _____

_____ Lastly, I am very

_____

To summarize, _____

_____

Task 5-9 — Self/Peer Revising/Editing

自分の（あるいはパートナーの）パラグラフについて、以下の点をチェックしましょう。

Paragraph Level Check Points

- The first few sentences introduce the general background of the topic. ☐ Yes ☐ Not sure ☐ No

- The paragraph has a topic sentence that tells the reader what the paragraph is about and what the writer wants to say about it. ☐ Yes ☐ Not sure ☐ No

- The paragraph has good supporting sentences that elaborate on the main idea by giving further explanations, reasons, or examples. ☐ Yes ☐ Not sure ☐ No
  There are (   ) supporting sentences.

- Transition words are used appropriately to make the organization clear. ☐ Yes ☐ Not sure ☐ No

- The paragraph has a good concluding sentence that paraphrases the topic sentence, summarizes the main points, or gives a final comment on the topic. ☐ Yes ☐ Not sure ☐ No

Sentence Level Check Points

Nouns
- Check if all the nouns are used appropriately, in their singular or plural forms, and with or without articles or other determiners.
  ☐ Done
  — found (   ) mistakes

Subject-Verb Agreement
- Check if the subjects and verbs agree in number.
  ☐ Done
  — found (   ) mistakes

Tense
- Check if the tenses of all the verbs are appropriate.
  ☐ Done
  — found (   ) mistakes

📖 Focusing on Form

Articles & Nouns

名詞は countable か uncountable かを常に意識することが必要です。また、冠詞その他の限定詞が必要か必要でないかも常に気にしましょう。

Now *you* try !

次のセンテンスは名詞がすべて単数形でかつ「裸」です。例にならい、必要に応じて語形を変えたり、語を補ったりしてください。

Ex) Parent should not force value on child.
    → Parents should not force **their** values on **their** child**ren**.

1. Doing sport is good way to get rid of stress.

2. If you do different kind of part-time job, you can get lot of different experience.

3. Having student evaluate instructor at end of semester is relatively new system.

4. It is unnerving to think that many animal are experimented on to test new cosmetic.

5. It is crucial to tell fact from opinion when you watch news program.

6. Internet news site affect way thinking before we know.

7. It is estimated that if world population keeps growing at current rate, it will double by year 2050.

8. There must be much more domestic violence than is reported to police.

9. People usually do not have chicken or cow in mind when they eat chicken or beef.

UNIT

6

Describing Your Daily Life
大学生活は大変？それとも楽チン？

このUnitでは自分の1週間の生活サイクルに対する
感想を述べるパラグラフを書きましょう。

Task 6-1 Generating Ideas

自分の1週間の生活サイクルを考えた時、それぞれの形容詞がどの程度当てはまるか、当てはまらないかに○をつけましょう。

extremely	very	rather	not very	not at all	
5	4	3	2	1	active
5	4	3	2	1	aimless
5	4	3	2	1	adventurous
5	4	3	2	1	boring
5	4	3	2	1	busy
5	4	3	2	1	carefree
5	4	3	2	1	demanding
5	4	3	2	1	dull
5	4	3	2	1	exciting
5	4	3	2	1	easy
5	4	3	2	1	easygoing
5	4	3	2	1	enjoyable
5	4	3	2	1	fruitful
5	4	3	2	1	fulfilling
5	4	3	2	1	hectic
5	4	3	2	1	idle
5	4	3	2	1	immoral
5	4	3	2	1	joyless
5	4	3	2	1	quiet
5	4	3	2	1	lazy
5	4	3	2	1	leisurely
5	4	3	2	1	lonely
5	4	3	2	1	miserable
5	4	3	2	1	peaceful
5	4	3	2	1	riotous
5	4	3	2	1	romantic
5	4	3	2	1	tough
5	4	3	2	1	wholesome
5	4	3	2	1	wild

Task 6-2 Talking in Pairs

ペアになり、Task 6-1 で選んだ形容詞を使って、次のような形でやり取りをしてみましょう。

A: How do you find your life now?
B: I should say ... it's _____ and [but] _____ .
A: _____ and [but] _____ ? In what way?
B: _____
   _____ .

Example 1

CD 14   DL 14

A: How do you find your daily life now?
B: I should say ... it's tough and demanding.
A: Tough and demanding? In what way?
B: Well, one English professor is unbelievably demanding. He gives us tons of homework every week. It's tough but I feel I am learning something.

Example 2

A: How do you find your daily life now?
B: I should say . . . it's easygoing and carefree.
A: Easygoing and carefree? In what way?
B: Well, I have classes only three days a week, so I have a lot of free time to enjoy going out with friends.

Task 6-3 Writing a Topic Sentence

現在の1週間の生活に対する印象を、次の形で表現しましょう。これが topic sentence のもとになります。

Example

My weekly schedule can be described as tough and demanding.

My weekly schedule can be described as _____ .

Task 6-4 Writing Introductory Sentences

Topic sentence に読者を導くための introductory sentences を書きましょう。topic sentence よりも general な内容で始め、topic sentence につながるよう工夫します。

Example

People tend to have stereotypes. <general>

One such image may be a university student whose life is full of "all play and no work." <specific>

That image, however, is far from correct in my case. <more specific>

Actually, my weekly schedule can be described as tough and demanding.

Task 6-5 Outlining

自分の1週間の典型的な行動をメモの形にまとめましょう。

	Typical Activities		
	Morning	Afternoon	Evening
Mon.			
Tues.			
Wed.			
Thurs.			
Fri.			
Sat.			
Sun.			

Task 6-6 Writing Supporting Sentences

Task 6-5 で記入した表を見ながら、曜日を追って、主な活動を書きましょう。その際、Task 6-3 で書いた topic sentence をサポートする内容を中心的にピックアップしましょう。

次の表現が利用できます。

・On（曜日）, I have（科目名）.
・（科目名）is tough / okay / easy because ＿＿＿＿＿＿＿＿＿＿.
・（曜日）is my favorite day, because I have ＿＿＿＿＿＿＿＿＿＿＿.
・（曜日）is the toughest day for me because ＿＿＿＿＿＿＿＿＿＿.
・（曜日）is my least-favorite day. That is because ＿＿＿＿＿＿＿＿＿＿.
・I usually go out drinking / singing / dancing with friends on（曜日）evening.
・I work as a ＿＿＿＿＿＿＿ at a(n) ＿＿＿＿＿＿＿＿ for ＿＿＿＿＿ hours on（曜日）.

Example

・On Tuesday, I have Basic Programming, Psychology, and English.
・Phychology is tough because I get lots of reading assignments.
・Monday is my least-favorite day, because I have to switch from play to work mode.
・Thursday is the toughest day when I have five classes.
・Friday is the toughest day for me because of the English class in the morning.
・I usually go out drinking and singing with friends on Friday evening.
・I work as a waiter at a nearby restaurant for three hours on Monday, Tuesday, and Wednesday nights.

Task 6-7 Writing Concluding Sentences

Unit 4 で学んだ３つのテクニークで、concluding sentence を書いてみましょう。

Example

Technique 1 (Paraphrasing the topic sentence):
　　In this way, I am now leading a quite hard and challenging life.

Technique 2 (Summarizing the main points):
　　Thus, what makes my week tough and demanding is, in particular, the

amount of homework I have to do for the English class on Friday.

Technique 3 (Giving a final thought):

I sometimes envy my carefree friends, but I also believe working this hard will do me good in the long run.

Task 6-8　Putting It All Together

いままで書いた文を改めてパラグラフにまとめましょう。文と文の関係を明確にするためのつなぎ言葉も使いましょう。

Example

My Tough Weekly Schedule

People tend to have stereotypes. One such image may be a university student whose life is full of "all play and no work." That image, **however**, is far from correct in my case. Actually, my weekly schedule can be described as tough and demanding. It is as if my week starts on Friday afternoon and ends at noon on Friday. What makes me feel like that is one English class I have on Friday mornings. In that class, we have to be paying full attention to the professor all through the 90-minute session because anyone can be called on to answer a question at any minute. **What is more**, he rates every single response we make! Dozing off is just impossible. When the class is over, I feel exhausted and relieved. **However**, that feeling lasts only for about a day. On Saturday, I have to begin preparing for the next Friday's class. **In this way**, I am now leading a quite hard and challenging life. I sometimes envy my carefree friends, but I also believe working this hard will do me good in the long run.

Task 6-9 — Self/Peer Revising/Editing

自分の（あるいはパートナーの）パラグラフについて、以下の点をチェックしましょう。

Paragraph Level Check Points

- The first few sentences introduce the general background of the topic. ☐ Yes ☐ Not sure ☐ No

- The paragraph has a topic sentence that tells the reader what the paragraph is about and what the writer wants to say about it. ☐ Yes ☐ Not sure ☐ No

- The paragraph has good supporting sentences that elaborate on the main idea by giving further explanations, reasons, or examples. ☐ Yes ☐ Not sure ☐ No There are ( ) supporting sentences.

- Transition words are used appropriately to make the organization clear. ☐ Yes ☐ Not sure ☐ No

- The paragraph has a good concluding sentence that paraphrases the topic sentence, summarizes the main points, or gives a final comment on the topic. ☐ Yes ☐ Not sure ☐ No

Sentence Level Check Points

Nouns
- Check if all the nouns are used appropriately, in their singular or plural forms, and with or without articles or other determiners. ☐ Done — found ( ) mistakes

Subject-Verb Agreement
- Check if the subjects and verbs agree in number. ☐ Done — found ( ) mistakes

Tense
- Check if the tenses of all the verbs are appropriate. ☐ Done — found ( ) mistakes

Focusing on Form

Subject-Verb Agreement / Singular vs. Plural

言うまでもなく、主語と動詞の数は一致している必要があります。知識としては知っていても、実際に使えなければ意味がありません。

Now *you* try!

1〜9のセンテンスで使われている主語と動詞の対応はよいか、名詞は適当かを確認し、問題があれば直しましょう。ほかのタイプの誤りがある場合はそれも直しましょう。

1. France is one of the country that has nuclear weapons.

2. It is about one and a half year since I entered into this college.

3. I am not sure if everyone in class agree on this issue.

4. There is several reason why baseball are popular in Japan.

5. Most people says that watching sports in stadiums are the best way to enjoy, but is it a really true?

6. Not only watching games on internet but there is many way to make you exciting about sports.

7. The men in that black car was not dead but just slept.

8. Whoever say that I should quit, I will not. Because I don't want to be loser.

9. I am 18-year-old man who are planning to study abroad.

10. Reading is now one of the most interested hobby to me.

UNIT

7

Expressing an Opinion
歩きスマホやめてくれない？

この Unit では、自分の意見を述べるパラグラフを書いてみましょう。

Task 7-1　Generating Ideas

次のチャートを見て、自分の意見に比較的近いことを述べているセンテンスを5つ選んでください。選んだら、そう思う理由をひとつずつ考えてください。

〜するのは素晴らしい／馬鹿らしい

Prohibiting the use of Japanese in English classes Promoting diversity at workplaces Taking attendance at university classes Having students evaluate professors at the end of a semester Making English an official language of Japan	is an excellent idea. is an important idea. is a good idea. is not such a bad idea. is not such a good idea. is a bad idea. is a stupid idea.

〜を増やすべきだ／減らすべきだ

The number of	wheelchair-friendly facilities cafeterias at our university surveillance cameras in town compulsory subjects at our college smoke-free buildings and facilities gender-neutral toilets	has to be should be can be	increased. kept as it is. decreased.

許可されるべきだ／規制されるべきだ／禁止されるべきだ

Research on cloning people Making hate speech Smoking in restaurants Minors drinking Sexual harrassment	should be should not be	allowed. regulated. regulated more strictly. prohibited. penalized more severely.

〜人は素晴らしい／迷惑だ

People who	act to advance their political beliefs make steady efforts to realize their dreams are looking at their phones while walking don't try to stop minors from drinking do everything on their smartphones, without using PCs,	are admirable. are wonderful. should know better. are problematic. are pathetic. are annoying.

Task 7-2　Talking in Pairs

Task 7-1 で選んだセンテンスを利用して、ペアで話す練習をしてみましょう。

Example

A : Prohibiting the use of Japanese in English classes is an excellent idea.
B : Why do you think so?
A : Because we will not speak English if Japanese is not prohibited.
B : I see.

A : People who are looking at their phones while walking should know better.
B : Why do you think so?
A : It's a nuisance to other people.
B : I see.

Task 7-3　Writing a Topic Sentence

Task 7-2 で練習したセンテンスの中からひとつ選び、In my opinion, ... / I strongly believe that ... に続けて書きましょう。これが topic sentence となります。

Example

In my opinion, people who are looking at their phones while walking should know better.

Task 7-4　Writing Introductory Sentences

Topic sentence に読者を導くための introductory sentences を書きましょう。topic sentence よりも general な内容で始め、topic sentence につながるよう工夫します。

Example

To most people, smartphones have become something they cannot do without. <general>
Some never let go of their phones no matter when, where, and what they are doing.　<specific>
In my opinion, people who are looking at their phones while walking should know better.

Task 7-5 ▶ Outlining

Task 7-3 で書いた topic sentence の内容を読者に納得させるためのポイントを２つ以上考え、次のようなメモの形で書きましょう。この段階では英語表現に悩むより、内容的に説得力のある理由を立てることに集中してください。

Example

1. nuisance ... danger ... people around
2. drop phones ... damage
3. vulnerable ... crime .... snatcher

Task 7-6 ▶ Writing Supporting Sentences

Task 7-5 でたてたポイントのひとつひとつを、それぞれ２つのセンテンスで表現してください。最初のセンテンスは、比較的 general に、２番目のセンテンスは比較的 specific な内容にします。

Example

1. nuisance ... danger ... people around
   - They are a nuisance as well as a potential danger to people around them.
   - Other people have to step aside to let them through.

2. drop phones ... damage
   - They may drop their precious phones and damage them.
   - A friend of mine tripped when texting, and dropped his iPhone.

3. vulnerable ... crime
   - They can make themselves vulnerable to crime.
   - They can be easy prey for snatchers, muggers or even rapists.

Task 7-7 ▸ Writing Concluding Sentences

Unit 4 で学んだ 3 つのテクニックで concluding sentence を書いてみましょう。

Example

Technique 1 (Paraphrasing the topic sentence):
For these reasons, I strongly believe that people should not use their phones while walking.

Technique 2 (Summarizing the main points):
To summarize, people should not use their phones while walking because it annoys other people, can result in broken phones, and can make them end up crime victims.

Technique 3 (Giving a final thought):
Let there be no "smartphone-zombies" in town!

Task 7-8 ▸ Putting It All Together ● CD 17 ⬇ DL 17

いままで書いた文を改めてパラグラフにまとめましょう。構成を明確にするためのつなぎ言葉も使いましょう。

Why You Should Stop Looking at Your Phones While Walking

To most people, smartphones have become something they cannot do without. Some never let go of their phones no matter when, where, and what they are doing. But in my opinion, people who are looking at their phones while walking should know better. **First**, they are a nuisance as well as a potential danger to people around them. Other people have to step aside to let them through. What if they bump into elderly people and hurt them? **Second**, they may drop their precious phones and damage them. A friend of mine tripped when texting, and dropped his iPhone, which cost him 10,000 yen to fix. **Third**, they can make themselves vulnerable to crime. Since they are not looking at their surroundings, they can be easy prey for snatchers, muggers or even rapists. **To summarize**, people should not use their phones while walking because it annoys other people, can result in broken phones, and can make them end up crime victims. Let there be no "smartphone-zombies" in town!

Task 7-9 — Self/Peer Revising/Editing

自分の（あるいはパートナーの）パラグラフについて、以下の点をチェックしましょう。

Paragraph Level Check Points

- The first few sentences introduce the general background of the topic. ☐ Yes ☐ Not sure ☐ No

- The paragraph has a topic sentence that tells the reader what the paragraph is about and what the writer wants to say about it. ☐ Yes ☐ Not sure ☐ No

- The paragraph has good supporting sentences that elaborate on the main idea by giving further explanations, reasons, or examples. ☐ Yes ☐ Not sure ☐ No
There are (　　) supporting sentences.

- Transition words are used appropriately to make the organization clear. ☐ Yes ☐ Not sure ☐ No

- The paragraph has a good concluding sentence that paraphrases the topic sentence, summarizes the main points, or gives a final comment on the topic. ☐ Yes ☐ Not sure ☐ No

Sentence Level Check Points

Nouns
- Check if all the nouns are used appropriately, in their singular or plural forms, and with or without articles or other determiners. ☐ Done — found (　　) mistakes

Subject-Verb Agreement
- Check if the subjects and verbs agree in number. ☐ Done — found (　　) mistakes

Tense
- Check if the tenses of all the verbs are appropriate. ☐ Done — found (　　) mistakes

Focusing on Form

Tenses

時制の種類は知っていても、どの時制をどこで使うべきか、を誤解している人が多いようです。特に過去形を使うべき時に過去完了や現在完了を使ってしまうミスや、あるいはその逆のミスなどが多く見られます。

Now *you* try!

次の１〜３は大学生が過去を振り返って書いたものです。時制の誤りがあれば直しましょう。他のタイプの誤りもあれば同時に直しましょう。

1. In my childhood, when I go to bed, Mother always sing a song.

2. I started school when I was four years old. I have been a student for sixteen years. I had studied Japanese, math, science, and so on in junior and senior high schools. I attend this university for one and a half year. I have been studied about information technology.

3. I had belonged to a swimming club when I was a high school student. I wanted to enter it in university. Therefore, since there is not it in this campus, I couldn't enter it. However, since I couldn't gave up entering it, now I am going to a swimming school near my apartment.

UNIT

8

Giving Advice and Instructions
ネットショッピング詐欺に引っかからないために

このUnitでは、「××の効果的な方法」「○○のやり方」など、物事の方法や手順について読み手にアドバイスするパラグラフを書きましょう。

Task 8-1 — Generating Ideas

まず何の方法について書くかを考えましょう。自分がよく知っていることがよいでしょう。決まらない場合は、次の中から選ぶこともできます。

- How to Find a Boy/Girlfriend
- How to Make Friendship Last Long
- How to Work Part-Time Successfully
- How to Survive Professor X's course
- How to Make Your Phone's Battery Last Longer
- How to Protect Your Money from Internet Shopping Scams

Task 8-2 — Writing a Topic Sentence

上で選んだトピックについて、次のような文を書きましょう。これが topic sentence のもとになります。

パタン A: _____ ing will be easy if you follow these steps.

パタン B: If you want to _____ , you should do the following.

パタン C: To _____ , there are some do's and don'ts.

Example

To protect your money from internet shopping scams, there are some do's and don'ts.

Task 8-3 — Writing Introductory Sentences

Topic sentence に読者を導くための introductory sentences を書きましょう。topic sentence よりも general な内容で始め、topic sentence につながるよう工夫します。

Example

- Online shopping enables you to buy almost anything from books to clothing to jewelry without leaving your home. <general>
- But that convenience comes at a price. <more specific>
- After you make your payment, you sometimes either receive fake items or receive nothing at all. <more specific>
- To protect your money from internet shopping scams, there are some do's and don'ts.

\<Peer Advising\>

ペアでお互いの Introductory sentences を検討し、流れが general → specific となっているかを確認し、必要に応じてサジェスチョンを行ないましょう。

Task 8-4 Outlining

Topic sentence をサポートするポイントを箇条書きにした outline を書きましょう。

Example

1. do not jump / too good a deal
   famous items / low price = fake
2. beware / strange language
   giveaways / scam websites / non-native speakers
3. payment methods
   ○ credit card / debit card / PayPal
   × money order / pre-paid card / bank transfer

Task 8-5 Talking in Pairs   CD 18   DL 18

Task 8-4 で書いた outline を利用して、ペアで話す練習をしてみましょう。

Example

A: If you want to protect your money from online shopping scams, there are some do's and don'ts. First, don't jump at deals that are too good to be true.
B: Too good to be true? What do you mean?
A: Famous branded items sold at too cheap a price must be fake.
B: That's true. Anything else?
A: Pay attention to the language used on the website. If you see grammatical mistakes or spelling mistakes, be careful.
B: Why?
A: Because that website is very likely to be a scam.
B: I see.
(*The interaction continues.*)

Task 8-6 ▶ Writing Supporting Sentences

Task 8-4 でたてたポイントのひとつひとつを、それぞれ２つ以上のセンテンスで表現してください。最初のセンテンスは、instruction（指示）に、２番目以降のセンテンスは reason にします。

1. do not jump to too good a deal
   famous items / low price = fake
   - Do not jump at deals that are too good to be true. <instruction>
   - Famous branded items advertised at unreasonably low prices are likely to be fake. <reason>

2. beware of strange language
   giveaways / scam websites / non-native speakers
   - Beware of misspellings and grammatical mistakes used on the site. <instruction>
   - These are often giveaways of scam websites created by nonnative speakers of the language. <reason>

3. payment methods
   ○ credit card / debit card / PayPal
   × money order / pre-paid card / bank transfer
   - Be alarmed if you are not allowed to pay through a secure service like credit card, debit card or PayPal. <instruction>
   - Once you make an up-front payment through a money order, pre-paid card, or bank transfer, your money is most likely lost forever. <reason>

Task 8-7 ▶ Writing Concluding Sentences

Unit 4 で学んだ３つのテクニークで concluding sentence を書いてみましょう。

Example

Technique 1 (Restating the topic sentence):
   Thus, these are three signs you should watch out for to protect your money from internet shopping scams.

Technique 2 (Summarizing the main points):
   To summarize, beware of too attractive a deal, watch out for strange

wording on the website, and avoid advance payment.

Technique 3 (Giving a final thought):

When in doubt, just Google the shop's name with the term "scam," which could save you a lot of money.

Task 8-8　Putting It All Together　CD 19　DL 19

いままで書いた文を改めてパラグラフにまとめましょう。構成を明確にするためのつなぎ言葉も使いましょう。

How to Protect Your Wallet from Online Shopping Scams

Online shopping enables you to buy almost anything from books to clothing to jewelry without leaving your home. But that convenience comes at a price. After you make your payment, you sometimes either receive fake items or receive nothing at all. To protect your money from internet shopping scams, there are several signs you should watch out for. First, do not jump at deals that are too good to be true. Famous branded items advertised at unreasonably low prices are likely to be fake. Second, beware of misspellings and grammatical mistakes used on the site. These are often giveaways of scam websites created by nonnative speakers of the language. Third and most important, be alarmed if you are not allowed to pay through a secure service like credit card, debit card or PayPal. Once you make an up-front payment through a money order, pre-paid card, or bank transfer, your money is most likely lost forever. In summary, beware of too attractive a deal, watch out for strange wording on the website, and avoid advance payment. When in doubt, just Google the shop's name with the term "scam." That one click could save you a lot of money.

Task 8-9 — Self/Peer Revising/Editing

自分の（あるいはパートナーの）パラグラフについて、以下の点をチェックしましょう。

Paragraph Level Check Points

- The first few sentences introduce the general background of the topic.　☐ Yes ☐ Not sure ☐ No

- The paragraph has a topic sentence that tells the reader what the paragraph is about and what the writer wants to say about it.　☐ Yes ☐ Not sure ☐ No

- The paragraph has good supporting sentences that elaborate on the main idea by giving further explanations, reasons, or examples.　☐ Yes ☐ Not sure ☐ No
There are (　) supporting sentences.

- Transition words are used appropriately to make the organization clear.　☐ Yes ☐ Not sure ☐ No

- The paragraph has a good concluding sentence that paraphrases the topic sentence, summarizes the main points, or gives a final comment on the topic.　☐ Yes ☐ Not sure ☐ No

Sentence Level Check Points

Nouns
- Check if all the nouns are used appropriately, in their singular or plural forms, and with or without articles or other determiners.　☐ Done　— found (　) mistakes

Subject-Verb Agreement
- Check if the subjects and verbs agree in number.　☐ Done　— found (　) mistakes

Tense
- Check if the tenses of all the verbs are appropriate.　☐ Done　— found (　) mistakes

Focusing on Form

Run-Ons

２つ以上のセンテンスを単にコンマでつないで１つのセンテンスのようにしたもの (Run-ons) は誤りです。適切な接続詞でつなぐ必要があります。

× A famous branded bag is sold very cheaply, that is likely to be a fake.
○ If a famous branded bag is sold very cheaply, that is likely to be a fake.
○ When a famous branded bag is sold very cheaply, that is likely to be a fake.

次のような形も可能です。
○ A famous branded bag sold very cheaply is likely to be a fake.

Now *you* try!

次の１～４の中に、Run-Ons があれば適切に直しましょう。

1. At high school, teachers tell you what to do and what not to do, at college, you can do anything you like.

   _____

2. I work part-time, I do not have to be totally dependent on my parents.

   _____

3. The current rate of fertility does not change, world population will double by the year 2050.

   _____

4. Sports cars have good acceleration, they get poor mileage.

   _____

UNIT

9

Comparing and Contrasting
似て非なるもの：パブと居酒屋

この Unit では、似ているけれど違う二つのものを比較対照する
パラグラフを書いてみましょう。

Task 9-1 Generating Ideas

まず何と何を比較するかを考えましょう。あまり一般に指摘されていない違いがあるものがよいですね。決まらない場合は、次の中から選ぶこともできます。

- High School Teachers and University Professors
- My Best Friend and I
- Windows and Macintosh
- iPhones and Android phones
- Professor A and Professor B
- Kansai People and Kanto People
- Living With Your Family and Living by Yourself

Task 9-2 Writing a Topic Sentence

上で選んだトピックについて、次のような文を書きましょう。これが topic sentence のもとになります。

パタン A: _____ and _____ are different [similar] in several (interesting / amusing / important) ways.

パタン B: _____ is different from [similar to] _____ in several (interesting / amusing / important) ways.

Example

A pub is different from a Japanese *izakaya* in several interesting ways.

Task 9-3 Writing Introductory Sentences

Topic sentence に読者を導くための introductory sentences を書きましょう。topic sentence よりも general な内容や、個人的なエピソードで始め、topic sentence につながるよう工夫します。

Example

I had a chance to live in the UK from 2016 to 2017. <personal episode>
During that period, I learned a lot about British culture, the most interesting of which was about pubs. <general → specific>
A pub is different from a Japanese *izakaya* in many interesting ways.

<Peer Advising>
ペアでお互いの Introductory sentences を検討し、うまく reader を topic sentence に導けているかを確認し、必要に応じてサジェスチョンを行ないましょう。

Task 9-4 Outlining

Topic sentence をサポートするポイントを箇条書きにした outline を書きましょう。

Example

1. how to buy drinks
   pub: go to the bar / buy / bring to seat
   izakaya: attendant comes to seat / takes order
2. standing vs. sitting
   pub: keep standing / empty seats available
   izakaya: sit at tables
3. food
   pub: few order food / just drink without eating
   izakaya: order a variety of food

Task 9-5 Talking in Pairs   CD 20   DL 20

Task 9-4 で書いた outline を利用して、ペアで話す練習をしてみましょう。

Example

A : Do you know how a British pub is different from a Japanese *izakaya*?
B : A pub and an *izakaya*? I am not very sure. Tell me.
A : Well, the first difference is in how you buy drinks. In a pub, you go to the bar, buy your drink, and bring it back to your seat. On the other hand, in an *izakaya*, ...
B : You stay at the table and an attendant will come to take your order.
A : Exactly. Another difference is whether people stand or sit.
B : What do you mean?
(*The interaction continues.*)

Task 9-6 ▸ Writing Supporting Sentences

Task 9-4 でたてたポイントのひとつひとつを、それぞれ２つ以上のセンテンスで表現してください。比較しているそれぞれの特徴をそれぞれ触れるようにします。

Example

1. how to buy drinks
   pub: go to the bar / buy / bring to seat
   izakaya: server comes to seat / takes order

- In a pub, you go to the bar, buy your drink, and bring it back to your seat.
- In an *izakaya*, a server will come to your seat, take your order, and then bring it to you.

2. standing vs. sitting
   pub: keep standing / empty seats available
   izakaya: sit at tables

- In a pub, a lot of people keep standing even when there are empty seats available.
- In an *izakaya*, everyone will be sitting at tables.

3. food
   pub: few order food / just drink without eating
   izakaya: order a variety of food

- In a pub, few people order food. Most people just drink beer without eating anything at all.
- In an *izakaya*, everyone will order a variety of dishes to enjoy with their drinks.

Task 9-7 ▸ Writing Concluding Sentences

Unit 4 で学んだ３つのテクニックで、concluding sentence を書いてみましょう。

Example

Technique 1 (Restating the topic sentence):
   Thus, there are intriguing differences between a pub and an *izakaya*.

Technique 2 (Summarizing the main points):
   To summarize, a typical customer in a pub buys beer at the bar, keeps standing, and does not eat, while an *izakaya* customer orders at the table, keeps sitting, and eats a lot.

Technique 3 (Giving a final thought):

A pub is more relaxing while an *izakaya* is more lively. They are both enjoyable places in their own ways.

Task 9-8 Putting It All Together

いままで書いた文を改めてパラグラフにまとめましょう。構成を明確にするためのつなぎ言葉も使いましょう。また、文のパタンが単調にならないよう、センテンスの始まりに変化をつけましょう。

Example

The Pub and the *Izakaya*

I had a chance to live in the UK from 2016 to 2017. During that period, I learned a lot about British culture, the most interesting of which was about pubs. A pub is different from a Japanese *izakaya* in many interesting ways. **First of all**, in a pub, you go to the bar, buy your drink, and bring it back to your seat. In an *izakaya*, a server will come to your seat, take your order, and then bring it to you. I was also intrigued to see a lot of people who keep standing—for hours—in a pub, even when there are empty seats available. If you did that in an *izakaya*, you would appear a very strange person. **Finally**, few people order food in a pub. Most people just drink beer without eating anything at all. **On the other hand**, in an *izakaya*, everyone will order a variety of dishes to enjoy with their drinks. **Because of these differences**, a pub and an *izakaya* have somewhat different atmospheres. I would say that a pub is more relaxing while an *izakaya* is more lively. They are both enjoyable places in their own ways.

Task 9-9 — Self/Peer Revising/Editing

自分の（あるいはパートナーの）パラグラフについて、以下の点をチェックしましょう。

Paragraph Level Check Points

- The first few sentences introduce the general background of the topic. ☐ Yes ☐ Not sure ☐ No

- The paragraph has a topic sentence that tells the reader what the paragraph is about and what the writer wants to say about it. ☐ Yes ☐ Not sure ☐ No

- The paragraph has good supporting sentences that elaborate on the main idea by giving further explanations, reasons, or examples. ☐ Yes ☐ Not sure ☐ No
  There are (　　) supporting sentences.

- Transition words are used appropriately to make the organization clear. ☐ Yes ☐ Not sure ☐ No

- The paragraph has a good concluding sentence that paraphrases the topic sentence, summarizes the main points, or gives a final comment on the topic. ☐ Yes ☐ Not sure ☐ No

Sentence Level Check Points

Nouns
- Check if all the nouns are used appropriately, in their singular or plural forms, and with or without articles or other determiners. ☐ Done　— found (　　) mistakes

Subject-Verb Agreement
- Check if the subjects and verbs agree in number. ☐ Done　— found (　　) mistakes

Tense
- Check if the tenses of all the verbs are appropriate. ☐ Done　— found (　　) mistakes

📋 Focusing on Form

Choppiness (I)

あまりに短いセンテンスばかりを羅列すると、幼稚な印象を与えます。適切な従属接続詞や分詞構文等を使って、複文を作る努力が必要です。（注意：and, but, so などの等位接続詞だけで文をつないでも幼稚な印象は変わりません。）

Now *you* try ✏️

例にならって、次の1〜4のそれぞれに含まれるすべての情報を、1センテンスで表してみましょう。

Example: I forgot to put suntan lotion on my back. I got severely burned. I look like a piece of bacon.
→ Since I forgot to put suntan lotion on my back, I got severely burned and now look like a piece of bacon.

1. I am a Japanese woman. I am 19 years old. I am thinking of studying at a college in the U.K.

   _____

   _____

2. My hometown is Katsunuma. It is in Yamanashi. It is located about 120 km northwest of Tokyo. It is a beautiful city. It is famous for wine production.

   _____

   _____

3. My uncle is an interesting person. His name is Suzuki Takashi. He was born in Taiwan. He grew up in Russia. Now he lives in Osaka. He works in the secretariat of an NGO.

   _____

   _____

4. Dinosaurs dominated the earth for 140 million years. It was a long time. After that, they became extinct. What caused them to become extinct? What do you think?

_____

_____

UNIT

10

Explaining Japanese Culture
説明しよう、日本の文化

このUnitでは、日本の食べ物や習慣について
説明する練習をしましょう。

Task 10-1

次の表の食べ物、料理法、主な材料を線で結びましょう。

Food	Way of Cooking	Main Ingredient
A: *nikuyasai-itame*	raw	fish
B: *okonomi-yaki*	cooked in a shallow pan	beef
C: *sukiyaki*	steamed	pork
D: *tonkatsu*	deep-fried	chicken
E: *sashimi*	stir-fried	prawns
F: *nimono*	cooked on a griddle	vegetables
G: *tempura*	boiled	flour
		seafood

Task 10-2

CD 22　DL 22

音声あるいは先生の説明を聞き、Task 10-1 の A～G のうち、どの食べ物のことか当ててみましょう。

1	2	3	4	5	6	7

Task 10-3

CD 23　DL 23

ペアになり、ひとりが Task 10-1 の A～G に次の H～M を加えたなかから一つ選び、英語で説明します。パートナーは、説明を聞き、どの料理のことか当てます。交代しながら何度か繰り返しましょう。

| H. *yakizakana* | I. *yakiimo* | J. *shabushabu* | K. *oden* |
| L. *chaahan* | M. *gyudon* | | |

Example

A: This is simply raw fish. We eat a variety of fish in this style.
B: Do you mean *yakizakana*?
A: Wrong! It's raw. Think again.
B: Do you mean *sashimi*?
A: Bingo!

Task 10-4

Task 10-3 の練習にもとづいて、A～M の食べ物を説明するセンテンス（それぞれ1～3センテンス）を書いてみましょう。

A) *tonkatsu*

   Example: *Tonkatsu* is deep-fried pork, usually eaten with sliced cabbage.

B) *tempura*

C) *sukiyaki*

D) *nikuyasai-itame*

E) *sashimi*

F) *nimono*

G) *okonomi-yaki*

H) *yakizakana*

I) *yakiimo*

J) *shabushabu*

K) *oden*

L) *chaahan*

M) *gyudon*

Task 10-5

この他に自分の好きな日本の食べ物を説明するセンテンスを書いてみましょう。

Task 10-6

次の15のセンテンス（A～O）を、two introductory statements, one topic sentence, eleven supporting sentences, one concluding sentence から成るパラグラフに構成したいと思います。最も適当な順番を考え、またペアで検討しましょう。音声を聞いて正解を確認した後、全文を改めてパラグラフ形式で書きましょう。

Elements of a Typical Japanese Meal

A) A typical Japanese meal, on the other hand, consists of *gohan*, *okazu*, and *miso-shiru*.
B) Examples are *yakizakana*, or grilled fish, and *yakiniku*, or grilled beef.
C) Finally, *miso-shiru* is a traditional *shiru*, or soup, containing vegetables seasoned with *miso*, or bean paste.
D) If fish or meat is grilled, it is called *yakimono*.
E) If things are boiled, they are called *nimono*.
F) If things are deep-fried, they are *agemono*.
G) In every culture, a typical meal is made up of several elements.
H) In the West, the three basic elements are a starter, the main course, and dessert.
I) It is not seasoned, so it goes well with the second element, *okazu*.
J) Many Japanese feel a meal is not complete if any of these three elements, *gohan*, *okazu*, and *miso-shiru*, is missing.
K) *Okazu*, which are fish, meat, or vegetables cooked in a variety of ways, are usually richly seasoned.
L) The first element, *gohan*, or boiled rice, is the staple food.
M) The most famous example of this may be *tempura*, deep-fried prawns and vegetables.
N) Three main ways of cooking these are grilling, boiling, and deep-frying.
O) Vegetables are often boiled and seasoned with soy sauce.

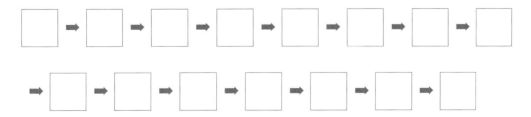

Task 10-7

左の事物と右の説明を結びましょう。正解は音声を聞いて確認しましょう。

1) *shichigo-san* ・ money given to children as presents at New Year's
2) *hanami* ・ an event in which people throw beans to drive away evil spirits
3) *tanabata* ・ a time in spring and autumn for us to remember our ancestors
4) *setsubun* ・ a party held under cherry blossoms
5) *o-toshidama* ・ an arranged date where single people who want to get married formally meet potential partners
6) *o-higan* ・ a festival to celebrate stars, which is held on July 7
7) *o-miai* ・ a festival to celebrate children who are turning seven, five, or three in the coming year

Task 10-8

ペアになり...

（1）A さんは Task 10-7 の右の説明部分を読み、パートナーが事物を当てましょう。

Example

A: What is the Japanese word for an event in which people throw beans to drive away evil spirits?
B: That's *setsubun*.

（2）A さんが Task 10-7 の左の事物を読み、パートナーが説明しましょう。

Example

A: What is *setsubun*?
B: It's an event in which people throw beans to drive away evil spirits.

Task 10-9

(1) 音声を聞き、1〜10が下の事物のどれのことを説明しているかを当てましょう。
(2) ペアになり、ひとりが下の事物のひとつを選んで英語で説明し、パートナーがどの事物かを当てる練習をしましょう。

1. _____ 2. _____ 3. _____ 4. _____ 5. _____
6. _____ 7. _____ 8. _____ 9. _____ 10. _____

hina-matsuri	koromo-gae	kanreki	tsukimi
ippon-jime	hikide-mono	o-mikuji	ema
miko	torii		

📖 Focusing on Form

Choppiness (II)

前Unitに引き続き、choppinessを直す練習です。

Now *you* try!

1〜4それぞれに含まれるすべての情報を、それぞれ1センテンスで表現してみましょう。

1. *Hanami* is a Japanese annual event. *Hanami* literally means blossom viewing. In this event, people hold wild parties. They do so under cherry blossom trees.

_____
_____
_____

2. The College Festival is held in autumn every year. It is an important occasion for students. The members of our club spend a long time preparing for it.

   _____

   _____

   _____

3. I argue that smoking should be banned in all public places. I argue so for several reasons. The most important reason is this. Secondhand smoke affects the health of others.

   _____

   _____

   _____

4. People in the West have a stereotype about the Japanese. The stereotype is that the Japanese are a diligent nation. It is also that they are difficult to understand. This movie reinforces that stereotype.

   _____

   _____

   _____

UNIT 11

Describing Data Expressed in Graphs
データにみる世界の現状

この Unit では、図や表から情報を読み取って
パラグラフを書く練習をしましょう。

社会でどの程度女性が活躍しているかは、国によってかなり違いがあるようです。図1（Figure 1）から情報を読み取り、質問に full sentence で答えると次のようになります。

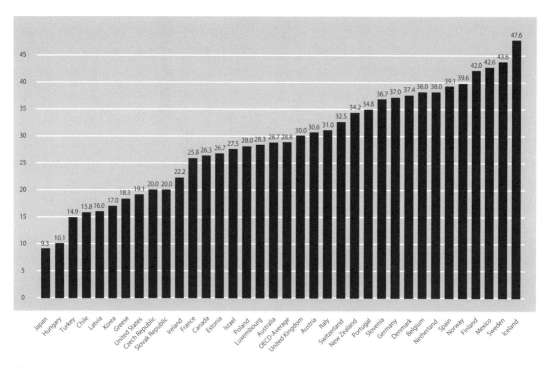

Figure 1. Women in politics: Percentages of women parliamentarians in 35 OECD countries (2017) (Source: OECD (2018), Women in politics (indicator). doi: 10.1787/edc3ff4f-en)

Example

1. **What does Figure 1 show?**
   — Figure 1 shows percentages of women parliamentarians in 35 OECD countries.

2. **In what order are the countries arranged from left to right?**
   — The countries are arranged from left to right in the ascending order of the percentages.

3. **How much do the percentages vary, from what figure to what figure?**
   — The percentages vary enormously from 9.3 to 47.6.

4. **What country is at the far left end with what percent of its Diet members being female?**
   — At the far left end of the graph is Japan, with only 9.3 percent of its Diet members being female.

5. **What is the OECD average? One out of how many is a woman across these countries?**
   — The OECD average is 28.8 percent, that is, one out of three parliamentary members is a woman across these countries.
6. **What country is at the far right end with what figure, followed by what countries with what figures?**
   — At the far right end is Iceland (47.6 percent), followed by Sweden (43.6 percent), Mexico (42.6 percent) and Finland (42.0 percent).
7. **How can you summarize the data?**
   — To summarize, the proportions of women parliamentary members in the OECD countries vary greatly from 9.3 percent of Japan at the bottom to 47.6 percent of Iceland at the top.

以上の回答をつなぎ合わせてパラグラフを作りました。センテンス間のつながりをよりなめらかにするためにつなぎ言葉を使ったり、繰り返しを避けるために表現を変えたり、補ったりしています。上の回答と異なる部分に下線を引いてチェックしましょう。

CD 28   DL 28

Figure 1 shows percentages of women parliamentarians in 35 OECD countries. The countries are arranged from left to right in the ascending order of the percentages. It is almost shocking to see how enormously the percentages vary. At the far-left end of the graph is Japan, with only 9.3 percent of its Diet members being female. In fact, Japan is the only country listed here whose percentage figure is lower than 10. The OECD average is 28.8 percent, that is, one out of three parliamentary members is a woman across these countries. At the far right end are countries with the largest proportion of women parliamentarians. The country with the largest proportion is Iceland (47.6 percent), followed by Sweden (43.6 percent), Mexico (42.6 percent) and Finland (42.0 percent). To summarize, the proportions of women parliamentary members in the OECD countries vary greatly from 9.3 percent in Japan at the bottom to 47.6 percent in Iceland at the top.

開発途上国を援助するために先進諸国は経済援助を行なっています。Figure 2 から読み取れる情報について、下の質問に full sentence で答えましょう。

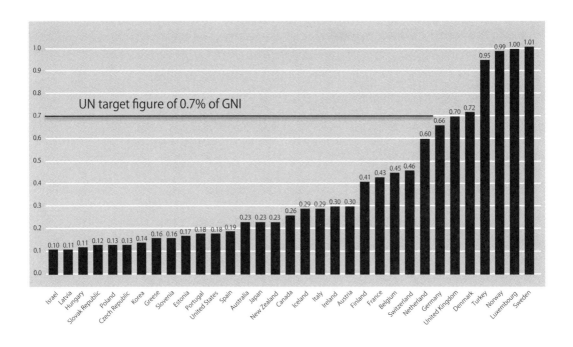

Figure 2. Official development assistance as a percentage of donor nation GNI, 2018 (Source: OECD (2018), Net ODA (indicator). doi: 10.1787/33346549-en)

1. What does Figure 2 show? What exactly do the numbers mean?

   _____

   _____

   _____

2. What is the target figure set by the United Nations?

   _____

   _____

   _____

3. By how many countries has that target figure been achieved or exceeded?

4. By which country has the highest figure been achieved, followed by which countries? What are their percentages?

5. What is Japan's figure? Which countries' is that same as?

6. Of all the countries, where is their percentage figure in the distribution?

7. Which country comes at the bottom at what percent? That is slightly exceeded by which countries at what percent?

8. How can you summarize the data?

_____

_____

_____

Task 11-2

🔘 CD 29　　⬇ DL 29

Task 11-1 の 1 〜 8 に対する答えをもとにパラグラフを書きましょう。センテンス間のつながりをよくするためにつなぎ言葉を使ったり、繰り返しを避けるために表現を変えたりすることに気をつけてください。解答例は音声を聞いて確認しましょう。

Task 11-3

世界ではどのくらいの割合の人が大学教育を受けて卒業するのでしょうか。Figure 3 から情報を読み取り、下の質問に full sentence で答えましょう。

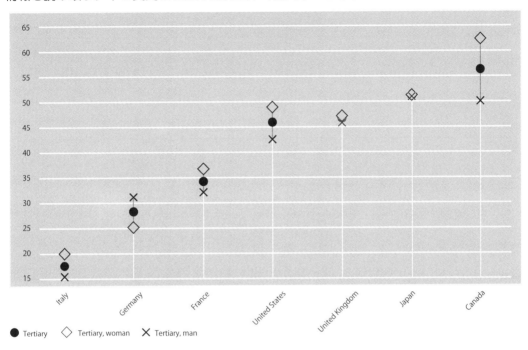

Figure 3. Percentages of men and women who complete tertiary education in G7 countries (Source: OECD (2018), Adult education level (indicator). doi: 10.1787/36bce3fe-en)

1. What does Figure 3 show?

   _____

   _____

2. Among the seven nations, are there considerable differences?

   _____

   _____

Unit 11: Describing Data Expressed in Graphs —— 87

3. What is the country with the highest percentage of people who complete university? That country is followed by what country and what country?

   _____
   _____

4. What is the country with the lowest figure and that with the second lowest figure?

   _____
   _____

5. What does the gender breakdown show? In which countries does a higher percentage of women than men complete tertiary education?

   _____
   _____

6. What was the gender difference like, in Japan as well as in the UK?

   _____
   _____

7. How can you summarize the data?

   _____
   _____

Task 11-4

Task 11-3 で書いたセンテンスをまとめてパラグラフにしてみましょう。その際、つなぎ言葉を使ったり、繰り返しを避けるために表現を変えたりすることに気をつけましょう。解答例は音声を聞いて確認しましょう。

世界の人口爆発は地球規模の深刻な問題です。世界の人口が21世紀末までにどう変わっていくかの予測について、Table 1 から 1 〜 4 の内容を読み取り、パラグラフを書きましょう。

Table 1. Population of the world and major areas, 2015, 2030, 2050 and 2100, according to the medium-variant projection

Major area	Population (millions)			
	2015	2030	2050	2100
World	7 349	8 501	9 725	11 213
Africa	1 186	1 679	2 478	4 387
Asia	4 393	4 923	5 267	4 889
Europe	738	734	707	646
Latin America and the Caribbean	634	721	784	721
Northern America	358	396	433	500
Oceania	39	47	57	71

Source: United Nations, Department of Economic and Social Affairs, Population Division (2015). *World Population Prospects: The 2015 Revision.* New York: United Nations.

1 2015年には世界人口は何人で、世界の地域ごとの分布の割合（パーセンテージ）はどうでしたか。

2 2015年〜2030年、2030年〜2050年、2050年〜2100年には、それぞれどのくらいの人口増が見込まれますか。

3 その結果2100年の世界人口は何人で、世界の地域ごとの分布の割合（パーセンテージ）はどうなると予測されますか。

4 2015年と2100年を比較して全体の人口増に大きく貢献するのはどの地域ですか。

人間が生きてゆく上で、安全な飲料水の確保はもっとも重要な課題の一つです。Figure 4 から読み取れる情報をもとに、世界でどのくらいの割合の人（その具体的な人数）が、どのような状態の飲料水の確保ができているのかについてパラグラフを書きましょう。とくにどのくらい人が、safely managed なレベルのサービスを、また、すくなくとも basic なレベルのサービスを享受できているのかを含んでください。人口の計算に際しては、Table 1 の数値を用いてください。

Figure 4. Proportion of population with different levels of drinking water services, 2015 (Source: JMP-2017-report-final.pdf)

📖 Focusing on Form

Parallel Structure

(both) A and B / (either) A or B / A, B, and C / A, B, or C などの構造において、A と B（および C）は、同等の文法構造をもつ（parallel である）必要があります。

Now *you* try!

例にならって、parallel でない部分を parallel に直しましょう。

Example: Ayaka is honest, kind, and has a warm heart.
→ Ayaka is honest, kind, and warm-hearted.

1. Two things that are particularly important to me are playing baseball and I like reading.

2. I really enjoy both skiing and the flute.

3. He is so attractive. Seeing him is to fall in love with him.

4. Whereas most married couples use the husband's family name, the wife's name is used in some cases.

5. At our university there are approximately 600 teachers and it has a clerical staff of 400.

6. Scientists now know how the disease is spread and about its prevention.

7. Their music is so cool, crazy, wild, and moves me.

UNIT

12

Summarizing What You Have Read
AIによって職が奪われるのか

この最後のUnitでは、読んだり聞いたりした内容を要約して
パラグラフにまとめる練習をしましょう。

Task 12-1

第三者の書いたものを報告する場合に気をつけるべきポイントが3つあります。音声あるいは先生の説明を聞き、メモしましょう。

CD 33 / DL 33 — Point 1

CD 34 / DL 34 — Point 2

CD 35 / DL 35 — Point 3

Task 12-2

つぎの "AI And The Future Of Work: Will Our Jobs Disappear?" を、要約することを念頭におきながら（内容的な key words に下線を引くなどしながら）読みましょう。

AI And The Future Of Work: Will Our Jobs Disappear?
Frida Polli

CD 36 / DL 36
1. "The sky is falling! The sky is falling!"

CD 37 / DL 37
2. Mainstream media has been consistently covering the negative discourse about AI and the future of work, with conversations often led by tech giants like Elon Musk and Bill Gates. We are living in a time that is reflective of the early 2000's. I remember a world of hysteria and bunkers filled with food, insurance, and so on.

CD 38 / DL 38
3. There seems to be something missing within the argument that there will be no jobs in the future due to AI. Elon Musk and Bill Gates are both brilliant and hugely successful CEOs, but neither trait speaks specifically to their foresight. The people we should be turning to to answer this problem are historians and futurists.

4. One of the most convincing technologists and futurists, Ray Kurzweil, says we have nothing to fear but fear itself. He explains that we have already eliminated all jobs several times over the course of history. This was accomplished with various disruptive technologies, be it the printing press, the steam engine or the automobile. Today's cycle is neither new nor catastrophic.

5. In 1900, two-thirds of the population worked in agriculture or manufacturing, with 38% on farms, and 25% in factories; Today, 1 in 10 do, with 2% and 9% respectively. Does that mean that 50% of the population is unemployed? Absolutely not! We have created hundreds and thousands of jobs that never existed.

6. The same sentiment goes for the future. Yes, the 3.1 million people that drive cars and trucks may eventually have their jobs eliminated. However, these eliminated jobs will certainly be replaced by industries and concepts that are yet to exist.

7. A job is defined as a piece of work for an agreed upon price. If we look around at the world today, are all of the tasks that need doing close to being accomplished? Not quite. War, poverty, discrimination, inequality, inefficiency, hunger, and slow food delivery… all of these massive problems continue to exist, and these large issues give way to equally large opportunities for people to find work. Does AlphaGo have the solution to these massive and intractable problems? If only that were the case.

8. An intriguing number of CEOs are convinced that humans will be replaced by machines. Instead of seeing this as inevitable, we need to see this as optional. Executives at blue-chip companies will have a choice to make – focus on cost-cutting or focus on creativity and quality.

9. Take the example of Accenture. They had 20,000 people employed in a job type that was prone to repeatable activities. Accenture challenged these employees to find a way to use technology to automate parts of their job, and if they did so, they would actually promote them to higher value activities. An amazing 60% of those employees' jobs were automated away by the employees themselves! Not a single person was made redundant. Instead, they all now work on higher value activities. Contrast this approach with the many companies that believe that if a job is automatable,

the person is no longer needed.

10. Gina Rometti, CEO of IBM, offers a more utopian and nuanced view. She makes the case that jobs will be changed by AI, but not replaced by AI. It is not man or machine. It is, as it has been since the invention of the first stone tool, man *and* machine. Take physicians, specifically radiologists, as an example. AI now can detect tumors on an X-ray. Can they do it better than humans? In some cases, yes. What the research actually shows is that AI is better at detecting some types of tumors, while doctors are better at detecting other types. The solution: Doctor + AI, neither one in isolation. This is at the heart of the term Intelligence Augmentation (IA) rather than Artificial Intelligence (AI).

（この部分は音声のみです）

(From Forbes.com, 2018/03/20 © Forbes. All rights reserved. Used by permission and protected by the Copyright Laws of the United States. The printing, copying, redistribution, or retransmission of this Content without express written permission is prohibited.)

Task 12-3

パラグラフ1～7の内容をひとつのパラグラフにまとめてみました。オリジナルと対照して、以下の点をチェックしましょう。

(1) 各センテンスがオリジナルの論文のどの部分に対応しているか、
(2) オリジナルの表現をどのように変えているか、
(3) 第三者が書いたものの要約である、あるいは直接引用である、ということをどのような表現で伝えているか。

The coverage in the media of AI and the future of work has been mostly negative, a common argument being that AI will take away jobs from us. Frida Polli argues, however, that that will not be the case. She cites technologist and futurist Ray Kurzweil, who reassures us that there is nothing to fear. That is because all jobs have, in history, already been eliminated several times over. For example, in 1900 the percentage of the population working at farms or factories was 63; today it is only 11. But that did not make 50% of the people unemployed because new jobs have been created. Similarly, though it may be true that car and truck drivers will eventually be made redundant, Polli argues, there will be new, unseen, types of jobs created instead. She also invites us to have a broader perspective on work. Defining a job as "a piece of work for an agreed upon price," she reminds us that there are a huge number of difficult problems to be solved in this world. That means, there will be huge opportunities to find work.

Task 12-4

パラグラフ 8 〜 10 を読み、パラグラフ 11 〜 13 の音声を書き取った上で、次の質問に対する答えを full sentence で書いてみましょう。

1. According to Polli, how many paths are there for big companies to choose from?

   _____

   _____

2. Big companies can focus on either what or what?

   _____

   _____

3. What company does Polli cite as a case that has succeeded in enhancing creativity and quality?

4. What did the company do, resulting in what?

5. Who is another executive who does not believe in replacing employees with AI?

6. According to Rometti, what will happen to jobs due to AI?

7. Will it be "man or machine" or "man *and* machine"?

8. In the field of radiology today, which can detect tumors the best, doctors only, AI only, or doctors plus AI?

9. At the heart of what concept is the combination of human and machines?

Task 12-5

Task 12-4で書いたセンテンスをまとめてパラグラフにしてみましょう。その際、つなぎ言葉を使ったり、繰り返しを避けるために表現を変えたりすることに気をつけましょう。解答例は音声を聞いて確認しましょう

Task 12-6　　　　　　　　　　　　　　　　　　CD 50　　DL 50

パラグラフ 11 〜 13 を、先生の説明または音声で聞いてメモをとり、それをもとにつぎの質問に対する答えを full sentence で書いてみましょう。

1. According to the WEF chairman, what will the key traits to the future of work be?

   _____

2. What are the three such traits cited?

   _____

3. What does Polli suggest we should not do?

   _____

4. What does Polli suggest we should do?

   _____

Task 12-7　　　　　　　　　　　　　　　　　　CD 51　　DL 51

Task 12-6 で書いた解答を、パラグラフの形にまとめましょう。

Focusing on Form

Miscellaneous

総仕上げとして、さまざまなタイプの誤りを含む文の editing を練習します。

Now *you* try!

1〜17のセンテンスの中に誤りがあれば直しましょう。いままで練習してきたタイプの誤りも、そうでないタイプの誤りも含まれています。

1. Parents don't have the right that put pressure on their children.

2. Formula One is a very dangerous car race but some parts of it make people very exciting.

3. Perhaps many students enter a college not decide to what they want to do.

4. He became a drinker as a result of unemployed.

5. What is particularly important to me is the time spending with my friends.

6. Almost people will say that I'm heavy too much. I planning to go diet one of these days.

7. Some friends of mine always chat about what I do not know topic, so I cannot stand to be with them.

Unit 12: Summarizing What You Have Read —— 101

8. One group of experts believes that global warming is part of the natural cycle of the earth, which there is nothing we can do.

9. High fertility because women can't control their reproductive lives results to population growth.

10. In the future, I believe many people will look things from different perspective, and that will make change in Japanese society.

11. I have ever experienced the same trouble as yours. I suggest that you discuss about it with your girlfriend.

12. How tiring I am, I never fail to go to work.

13. It seems difficult that we handle problem of sexual harassment. Because it is difficult that we define sexual harassment and there are many notions about sexual harassment.

14. The dog seems boring because he do not have a friend and he is alone.

15. During the first couple of months at this university, I didn't enjoy. Because I had no one to talk to.

16. If you have a pain in your elbow, why not stop playing tennis? Instead, you could play another sports what you don't need to use your right elbow.

17. Most of children don't go to school are girls and most live in Africa and South Asia.

Appendix: Additional Cues for Writing

People
1. What are the qualities of good parents?
2. Describe your appearance. What do you like most about the way you look? What features do you want to change?
3. Take two members of your family or two friends, and compare them. What are some of the differences and the similarities?
4. When you have a problem, whose advice do you seek most often, and why?
5. Do you agree or disagree with the following statement. "A man and a woman can never be friends." Give specific reasons and examples to support your answer.
6. Do you agree or disagree with the following statement? The first impression of a person is sometimes very different from what he/she really is. Give specific reasons and examples to support your answer.

Food
7. If you knew that the world is coming to an end (for whatever reason) today, what would you like to eat for your last meal?
8. What is your favorite dish? Explain what it is like and how to prepare it assuming the reader is a non-Japanese person.
9. Which do you prefer, dining at restaurants or having dinner at home? Give specific reasons and examples to support your answer.
10. Nowadays, many more types of ready-made foods are available at supermarkets and convenience stores than before. Has this change improved the way people live? Give specific reasons and examples to support your answer.

Places
11. What is your favorite place to spend a one-day holiday?
12. A person you know is planning to move to your town or city. What do you think this person would like and dislike about living in your town or city? Why?
13. Describe your favorite restaurant. What are the food, the service, and the

decor like?
14. Which do you think is better, to live in a big city or in a small town? Give specific reasons and details to support your answer.

Sports and Entertainment
15. What are some sports that you would like to try some day?
16. What are some of the sports that you would never want to try?
17. Describe a good movie that you watched recently. What did you like about it?
18. Some people prefer Japanese songs to English songs. Other people prefer English songs to Japanese songs. Which type are you?
19. People have different ways of getting rid of stress. Some read; some exercise; others play computer games. What is your favorite way? Give specific details and examples in your answer.
20. When you watch a movie, do you prefer to watch it in a movie theater or at home as a video?
21. Do you agree or disagree with the following statement? Movies and TV programs substantially affect how people behave. Give specific reasons and examples to support your answer.
22. Do you agree or disagree with the following statement? TV programs are spending too much time covering personal lives of celebrities. Give specific reasons and examples to support your answer.
23. Do you agree or disagree with the following statement? Generally speaking, foreign movies are more interesting than Japanese movies. Give specific reasons and examples to support your answer.

Lifestyle
24. What do you do every day? Describe your typical day. How do you find your daily schedule?
25. What do you like to do in your free time?
26. Some people prefer to get up early in the morning and start the days work. Others prefer to get up later in the day and work until late at night. Which do you prefer? Use specific reasons and examples to support your choice.
27. Some people prefer to spend most of their time alone. Others like to be with friends most of the time. Which type are you? Give specific reasons to support your answer.

28. In the next twenty years, what changes do you think will take place in society?
29. What imaginary invention would you like to have to improve your life?
30. In your opinion, what was the greatest invention in human history?
31. What does the following proverb mean? A rolling stone gathers no moss. Do you agree or disagree with the idea?
32. What does the following proverb mean? Every cloud has a silver lining. What do you think of the idea expressed in it?
33. Do you agree or disagree with the following statement? Telling a lie is sometimes a good thing. Give specific reasons and examples to support your answer.

School and Education
34. What are the qualities of a good university?
35. What are the qualities of a good university student?
36. What are the qualities of a good university teacher?
37. If you are to cite three good points of your university, what are they?
38. If you are to cite three bad points of your university, what are they?
39. There are classes where the teacher does most of the talking, as well as those where students discuss various issues. Which type of class do you prefer?
40. When an examination is drawing near, do you prefer to study alone or together with your friends?
41. Do you agree or disagree with the following statement? If there were no examinations or required papers, students would not study as much. Give specific reasons and examples to support your answer.
42. Do you agree or disagree with the following statement? Whether a student comes to like or dislike a certain school subject depends a lot on who is teaching it. Give specific reasons and examples to support your answer.
43. Do you agree or disagree with the following statement? Being a university student is a tough business. Give specific reasons and examples to support your answer.
44. Do you agree or disagree with the following statement? Universities should ask students to evaluate their teachers. Give specific reasons and examples to support your answer.

45. Do you agree or disagree with the following statement? High schools should ask students to evaluate their teachers. Give specific reasons and examples to support your answer.
46. Do you agree or disagree with the following statement? Primary schools should ask pupils to evaluate their teachers. Give specific reasons and examples to support your answer.
47. Do you agree or disagree with the following statement? Universities should admit anyone willing to study, without any screening. Give specific reasons and examples to support your answer.
48. Do you agree or disagree with the following statement? When learning something, it is always better to have a teacher. Give specific reasons and examples to support your answer.
49. If your university had an extra budget of five million yen, what do you think is the best way to spend it? Give specific reasons and details to support your choice.
50. Recall your high school and the days you spent there. If you could make one important change in the high school that you attended, what change would you make? Give reasons and specific examples to support your answer.
51. Some children spend a great amount of their time going to and studying at cram schools. Discuss the advantages and disadvantages of this. Use specific reasons and examples to support your answer.

Job

52. When choosing a job in the future, what features will be important to you? The pay level, flexibility of working time, creativity involved in the job, prestige associate with it, or something else?
53. Would you prefer joining and working for a large corporation or starting your own business?
54. Do you agree or disagree with the following statement? Everyone should retire at the age of 50 to give the post to a younger person. Give specific reasons and examples to support your position.

Animals and the Environment

55. Some people treat pets as members of their family. Do you think such a

relationship between humans and animals is a good one?

56. Do you agree or disagree with the following statement? It is wrong and disrespectful to keep animals in zoos. Give specific reasons and examples to support your answer.

57. Do you agree or disagree with the following statement? It is morally wrong to use animals in experiments to test the safety of such non-essential products as cosmetics. Give specific reasons and examples to support your answer.

58. Do you agree or disagree with the following statement? Human needs for development are more important than saving land for endangered animals. Give specific reasons and examples to support your answer.

59. Pets' lives are generally shorter than their owners'. Some people might want to have clones of their pets so that they can be accompanied by their loved ones all through their lives. Do you think this is acceptable?

Social Issues

60. In Japan, people are no longer allowed to smoke in many public places and office buildings. Do you think this is a good rule or a bad rule? Use specific reasons and details to support your position.

61. It has recently been announced that a new convenience store may be built right in front of your apartment (or house). Do you support or oppose this plan? Why? Use specific reasons and details to support your answer.

62. Even today, women are not allowed to step on a sumo-wrestling dohyo. Do you think this is a form of sexual discrimination that should be condemned or a tradition to be kept?

63. It is very common to see hundreds of bicycles left in front of, or near, railway stations. They block most of the sidewalks, so people have a hard time walking by. What are some solutions to this problem?

64. The population of Japan is slowly decreasing. What are the causes of this phenomenon, and what will be some consequences?

65. Today, Coming-of-Age-Day ceremonies are not what they used to be. There are countless reports of young participants disrupting the ceremonies by chatting, drinking, and even setting off fireworks during the speeches. What are some causes of this phenomenon and what are some solutions?

66. Today the legal age for drinking is twenty, but most university first-year students have opportunities to drink semi-legally. Do you think the legal age for drinking should be lowered?
67. Under the current system in Japan, married couples are required to use one and the same family name. Some people insist that the law should be revised so that married couple can retain two different family names if they wish to do so. What is your position on this issue?

| JPCA | 本書は日本出版著作権協会（JPCA）が委託管理する著作物です。
複写（コピー）・複製、その他著作物の利用については、事前にJPCA（電話 03-3812-9424, e-mail:info@e-jpca.com）の許諾を得て下さい。なお、無断でコピー・スキャン・デジタル化等の複製をすることは著作権法上の例外を除き、著作権法違反となります。 |
|---|---|
| 日本出版著作権協会
http://www.jpca.jp.net/ | |

Writing Facilitator: Introduction to Paragraph Writing **Revised Edition**
構造から学べるパラグラフ・ライティング入門【改訂版】

2019年4月10日　第1刷発行
2019年4月19日　第2刷発行

著　者　靜　哲人

発行者　森　信久
発行所　**株式会社　松 柏 社**
〒102-0072　東京都千代田区飯田橋1-6-1
TEL 03 (3230) 4813（代表）
FAX 03 (3230) 4857
http://www.shohakusha.com
e-mail: info@shohakusha.com

装　幀　小島トシノブ（NONdesign）
印刷・製本　中央精版印刷株式会社

ISBN978-4-88198-751-3
略号 = 751

Copyright © 2019 by SHIZUKA Tetsuhito
本書を無断で複写・複製することを禁じます。
落丁・乱丁は送料小社負担にてお取り替え致します。